POETRY MATTERS

Edited by Vivien Linton

Northern Ireland

First published in Great Britain in 2011 by:

 Young**Writers**

Remus House
Coltsfoot Drive
Peterborough
PE2 9BF
Telephone: 01733 890066
Website: www.youngwriters.co.uk

All Rights Reserved
Book Design by Samantha Wood
© Copyright Contributors 2010
SB ISBN 978-0-85739-285-5

Foreword

Since our inception in 1991, Young Writers has endeavoured to promote poetry and creative writing within schools by running annual nationwide competitions. These competitions are designed to develop and nurture the burgeoning creativity of the next generation, and give them valuable confidence in their own abilities.

This regional anthology is one of the series produced by our latest secondary school competition, *Poetry Matters*. Using poetry as their tool, the young writers were given the opportunity to tell the world what matters to them. The authors of our favourite three poems were also given the chance to appear on the front cover of their region's collection.

Whilst skilfully conveying their opinions through poetry, the writers showcased in this collection have simultaneously managed to give poetry a breath of fresh air, brought it to life and made it relevant to them. Using a variety of themes and styles, our featured poets leave a lasting impression of their inner thoughts and feelings, making this anthology a rare insight into the next generation.

Contents

Antrim Grammar School, Antrim

Philip White (11)	1
Kyra Parke (12)	1
Jack Sproston (11)	2
Bailey Wilson (12)	3
Edward Stirling (12)	3
Adam Simpson (12)	4
Kate Byrne (12)	4
Rory Sylvester (11)	5
Jamie Simpson (12)	6
Chloe Smyth (12)	6
Jessica Patterson (12)	7
Morgan Poots (11)	7
Aimee Wilding (11)	8
Freja Speedie (12)	9
Anna Wallace (12)	10
Rebecca Thompson (11)	10
David Porter (12)	11
Paul Cosby (11)	11
Philip Thompson (11)	12
Emma Carville (11)	12
Aaron Stevenson (11)	13
Hâf Bishop (12)	13
Naomi Clingen (11)	14
Jayne Clarke (12)	14
Josh Caldwell (11)	15
Mitchel Pearson (13)	15
Hannah Brown (12)	16
Jonathan Boyd (12)	16
Emily Bowman (12)	17
Caleb Allen (12)	17
Kyle Bainbridge (11)	18
Anna Nelson (11)	18
Jordan McKelvey (11)	19
Cameron McClurg (11)	20
Dale Morrow (11)	20
Victoria McKay (12)	21
Josh Kirkaldy (13)	21
Ryan Myles (12)	22
Steven Woolley (12)	22
Stephen Watt (13)	23
Daniel Pattinson (12)	24
Sophie Robinson (12)	25
Kristen Sinclair (13)	26
Tara Woodside (12)	28
Kate Peden (12)	29
Emma Olliver (13)	30
Jonathan Myles (12)	31
Lauren Wilson (12)	31
Victoria Clingen (12)	32
Stephen Houston (13)	33
Kimberley Fleming (14)	33
Ben Collister (12)	34
Rachel Cooke (12)	35
Ann Allen (12)	36
Emily Hunter (12)	37
Lucy Clarke (12)	38
Megan Hopkin (13)	39
Abbie Hylands (14)	40
Stephanie Houston (13)	41
Rachael Allen (13)	42
Cory Ponter (12)	43
Megan Ferry (14)	43
Matthew Lenehan (13)	44
Sophie Johnston (14)	45
Shannon Heaney (13)	45
Kathryn Jones (14)	46
Joshua Knight (14)	46
Sophie Hutchinson (14)	47
Quintin Higginson (13)	48
Rebecca Kennedy (14)	49
Emily Gamble (13)	50

Abigayle Gill [13]	51
Darren Glendinning [13]	52
Peter Mitchell [13]	54
Chloe McMullan [14]	55
Phil Magowan [13]	56
Yasmin Mirza [14]	57
Jack Lennon [13]	58
Karl McNeill [14]	59

Carrickfergus College, Carrickfergus

Matthew Braden [11]	60
Abby Adair [11]	60
Tamera Nicholl [12]	61
Iúri Sousa [12]	61
Sarah-Louise Boyd [11]	62
Tom Scott [12]	62
Stephen Cookson [11]	63
Tori Haughey [11]	63
Owen Shearer [11]	64
Peter Campbell [11]	64
Kyle McGookin [12]	65
David Alexander [11]	65
Sophie Mc'Clean [11]	66
Erin Gillies [12]	66
Christopher Wootton [11]	67
Alex Ogilby [11]	67
Natasha Millar [11]	68
Kurtis Hamilton [12]	68
Rachel Mathers [11]	69
Scott Laughlin [11]	69
Ethan Graham [11]	70
Jordan Spence [11]	71
Sophie McFall [11]	71
Rhiannon McFadden [11]	72
Abby Wilson [10]	72
James Sharples [11]	73
Dion Maguire [11]	73
Kane Brennan [11]	74
Owen MacLeod [12]	75
Joshua Mitchell [11]	76

Jordan Thompson [13]	76
Luke Fitzsimmons [13]	77
Kris Dines [14]	77
Andrew Campbell [13]	78
Kelly Brownlee [14]	78
Jennifer Hood [13]	79
Julianne Bailey [14]	80
Josh Mannis [12]	81
Jack White [12]	82
Ryan Jeavons [11]	82
Joshua Nicholson [13]	83
Colter Binnie [11]	83
Niall Douglas [13]	84
Gareth Smith [13]	84
Jonny Bingham [13]	85
Melissa Meldrum [13]	85
Kirstyn Ferris [14]	86
Glenn McKee [13]	86
Shannon Craney [13]	87
Rachel McVeigh [12]	88
Olivia Donaghy [11]	89
Matthew Dyer [11]	90
Ross McGinnis [13]	91

Carrickfergus Grammar School, Carrickfergus

Laura Webb [12]	92
Jamie Ross [12]	93
Emily Wilson [11]	93
Charlotte Majury [12]	94
Clara Rose Armstrong [11]	94
Aoife Burgess [11]	95
Kate McConnell [13]	95
Megan O'Callaghan [13]	96

Methodist College, Belfast

Ben Roddy [14]	107

Monkstown Community School, Newtownabbey
Jake McCullough [12] 107
Seliya Varghese [13] 108
Tylor Armstrong 109
Zara Tobin [11] 110
Taylor McGookin 110
James Wilson 111
James McClenaghan [12] 111
Jack Crowe [12] 112
Aaron Rea [13] 112
Ross Watters [14] 113
Sasha Tweedie 113
Amy Gilbert 114
Matthew Bell 115
Scott Wallace [13] 116
Luke Hope 116
Meghan Hope [12] 117
Nikita Bowers 118
Jasmin Younger [12] 119
Shannan Vicary [12] 120
Jake Peachey 121
Darren Downing [11] 122
Tammy Gourley [12] 123
Denika Cardwell [14] 124

St John's Business & Enterprise College, Dromore
Cillian McGoldrick [13] 125
Kirby Mullan [13] 126
Dean O'Neill [14] 127
Eimear Curran [13] 128
Deirbhla McNulty [13] 129

St Louise's Comprehensive College, Belfast
Kayleigh Wilson [13] 130
Megan Magee [13] 130
Holly McGurnaghan [14] 131
Nicole Millen [14] 131
Alisha Cully [13] 132
Aideen Macauley [13] 133

Cara Mulhern [13] 134
Caitlin Kelly [13] 134
Laura Fitzsimmons [12] 135
Ciara Thompson [14] 135
Siobhan Andrews [12] 136
Aoife McGuigan [12] 136
Niamh Jeffreys [14] 137
Mandy McManus [13] 138
Kerry Murray [13] 139
Sarah Mulholland [12] 140

St Mary's High School, Lurgan
Orlagh Headley [12] 140
Shannon Creaney [12] 141
Caitlin Cassidy [12] 141
Amy Fitzpatrick [12] 142
Connie Callaghan [11] 143
Anna Conway [12] 144
Anna Daggett [11] 145
Hannah Abraham [11] 146
Megan Grimes [11] 146
Eimear Campbell [11] 147
Sarah Campbell [12] 147
Athena Donnelly [11] 148
Katie Catney [11] 148
Ellie Comac [11] 149
Caitlin Seeley [11] 149

St Patrick's Academy, Lisburn
Emily Dowds [12] 150
Shannon Barlow [13] 151
Conor Quinn [14] 152
Marie Therese Clenaghan [13] 153
Christy Cyriac [12] 153

Sullivan Upper School, Holywood
Peter Baker [12] 154
Courtney Dawson [11] 155
Luke Niblock [13] 156
Sophie Frazer [13] 156

Andrew Cave (12)	157
Eryn McAvoy (12)	157
Emily Boyd (11)	158
Jonny Betts (13)	159
Kerry Patterson (12)	159
Tom Parsons (12)	160
James Gibson (12)	160
Rory Harrison (12)	161
Medbh Henry (12)	161
Andrew Bell (12)	162
Zoë Gibson (12)	163
Annie McQuoid (12)	164
Patrick Moorhead (12)	165
Emma Luke (13)	166
Michael Parr (11)	166
James Stewart (11)	167
Robin Watts (12)	167
Harrison Bell (11)	168
Wajed Amin (12)	170
Rory Jemphrey (11)	170
Calum Cowan (12)	171
Jack Bruce (12)	171
Rachel Cormier (14)	172
Sarah Gordon (11)	172
Lucy Hollies (11)	173
Zara Goldstone (11)	174
Alex Gibson (11)	175
Joe Higginson (11)	176
Hannah Yeates (14)	177
Sarah Long (14)	178
Jack Torrens (13)	178
Joanna Gallagher (13)	179
Ewan Nelson (12)	179
James Stevenson (12)	180
Ross McKenna (14)	182
Lucy O'Sullivan (13)	184
Fergus Jemphrey (13)	184
Thomas Johnston (14)	185
Hannah Jackson (13)	186
Jemma Speers (13)	187
Alisha Burrell (13)	188
Andy Martin (13)	189
George Patterson (14)	190
Jack Preece (13)	191
Aimeé McConnell (14)	192
Conor McEvoy (13)	193
Lydia McQuoid (11)	194
Aaron Banyard (12)	194
Rachel McDougall (15)	195
Chris Moore (17)	196
Katie Ireland (11)	197
Stuart Collinson (13)	197
Callum Jeffrey (12)	198
Adam McAllister (12)	199
Grace Douglas (13)	200
Jennie Pitt (12)	201
David Anderson (13)	202
Jessica Chrishop (12)	203

The Poems

Roller Coaster

Walking through a theme park,
Looking from side to side,
You see a killer ride,
Your eyes light up.
Queuing up, your heart starts to race.
Sitting down, setting off
You start to think, *oh why, oh why?*
You increase in speed, wails ring out,
Then people start to scream and shout.
Up and down, right and left,
Upside down, loop-the-loop,
Before you know it the ride ends,
Once you get out you say to your friends,
'Again, again!'

Philip White (11)
Antrim Grammar School, Antrim

Happiness

The smiles on people's faces,
The laughter all around,
The eyes grow bright and shiny,
The best type of sound.
The sun gets brighter and brighter,
Happiness all around.

Kyra Parke (12)
Antrim Grammar School, Antrim

The Dragon Tail

In the thundery sky
There were five dragons
And one of them
Just screamed!

One of them got its tail cut off,
It fell from the sky.
It tried to get it
But it was too far away.

So in the morning,
One lucky child
Went outside and saw
The dragon tail!

It was lying there.
He went to pick it up
But suddenly a dragon warrior
Burst through a house.

He said, 'That tail is mine.'
He also said,
'I must return it.'
So he got the tail.

But it was too late,
The dragon had come
And taken it away,
So they just went back inside.

Jack Sproston (11)
Antrim Grammar School, Antrim

Homework

Homework, homework, homework,
So time consuming.
My days so gloomy,
Four or five to be done.
All done,
But more to come.

Bailey Wilson (12)
Antrim Grammar School, Antrim

School

School, school, school,
I hate school!
I have to go to you Monday,
Tuesday . . .
Wednesday . . .
Thursday . . .
And finally . . . Friday!
Oh Friday,
And after Friday . . .
Saturday - I like Saturday!
And then it's Sunday!
But the weekend goes so quickly!
And *(groan)* it's back to . . .
Monday!

Edward Stirling (12)
Antrim Grammar School, Antrim

Thunderstorms

Thunderstorms try to make us scared,
They try to make us frightened,
They try to make us jump,
And they try to make babies cry.

They are huge, loud bangs like a firework going off.
They make huge flashes, like a light bulb blowing.
Thunderstorm's flash looks like it's lighting up with anger.
Its anger rains down on us,
And it goes over and over again.

Adam Simpson (12)
Antrim Grammar School, Antrim

Dolphins

Dolphins are wonderful creatures,
But they are definitely not immature.
They would not like to live in a bin,
Because they would not be able to swim.

All of them are blue,
Even when there are two.
Dolphins live under the sea,
So them we barely see.

I really don't have a clue
What dolphins actually do,
So if you find out,
Make sure you shout.

Kate Byrne (12)
Antrim Grammar School, Antrim

An Unusual Tale

In the rumbling volcano,
Three dragons were fighting.
When they flew into the air,
The sky was streaked with lightning.

But then in the air
A burst of flame shot past,
Putting some trees on fire,
Really, really fast.

The villagers were scared
That their houses would get burned,
So they ran towards the dragons
But then they suddenly turned . . .

Because the dragons flew right at them,
Roaring and spouting flames everywhere -
But then the dragons were scared away by . . .
A giant bear!

The townsfolk thought the bear was a gift
Sent to them from the sky,
So they treated him like a god
And fed him with cakes and pies.

But the bear ate all the food
That they had after the dragon attack,
Then they all shouted,
'We would rather have the dragons back!'

Rory Sylvester (11)
Antrim Grammar School, Antrim

The Hidden Assassin

Tip-a-tap-a, tip-a-tap-a
Go the assassin's boots on the roof,
Watchful for approaching guards.

Suddenly a guard appears,
Sneaking quietly in the shadows.
Snick! goes the blade through the man's skull,
Silently letting the body drop.

Tip-a-tap-a, tip-a-tap-a
Go the assassin's boots
As he fades into the shadows,
Looking for another victim.

Jamie Simpson (12)
Antrim Grammar School, Antrim

My Friends

Some are tall
Some are small

Some are sporty
Some are arty

Some love shopping
Some love writing

We are all different in our own ways,
But having lots of friends
It's all the same.
Friends right now, friends forever.

Chloe Smyth (12)
Antrim Grammar School, Antrim

The Graveyard

Halloween night the graveyard lights up,
The cross is shining in the glowing moonlight.
People walking past, crying tears of sadness
For their lost ones in the graves.
The graveyard brings sadness and despair.
It is a very cold, lonely and Gothic place -
How I would love to be there!

Jessica Patterson (12)
Antrim Grammar School, Antrim

My Dog, Molly

Jack Russell terrier who couldn't be merrier.
Always crazy, you wouldn't call her lazy.
The postman opens the gate with fear
Because he's read the sign, *'Jack Russell Lives Here'*.

'Are you going for a walk?'
Is Molly's favourite call.
'We're going to the park -
Go and get your ball.'

A few hours later, we're home from the park,
My mom gives off, 'It's starting to get dark.'
Molly's curled up on my lap.
'Ssshh, I can't believe it, she's actually having a nap!'

Morgan Poots (11)
Antrim Grammar School, Antrim

My Family

We are an average family,
A total of four which makes us one.
My small sister, Ellie,
Creates amusement and fun.

My dad, he drives an ambulance,
Looks after the sick and ill,
He works so very hard,
But loves his job and thinks it's brill!

My mum, she works in an office
Helping people to find a career.
Her days are so long,
Yet she feels so very sincere.

We all enjoy our home
And everyone helps out.
We all pull together,
Otherwise Dad would give a shout!

Aimee Wilding (11)
Antrim Grammar School, Antrim

The Hole

She sat in a dark hole, not even a bug,
She had to get out or go insane.
The hole was deep and dark and damp.
She started to climb,
The wall crumbled and she fell.
She tried to think what to do.
Call for help?
Sit and wait?
Maybe dig?
She was thinking when . . .
Drip-drop, drip-drop,
It's raining, oh no!
If the hole filled with water . . .
She couldn't swim!
Would she see anyone again?
When, 'Hello, is anyone there?'
Came from above.
'Yes, can you help me?'
Down came the rope.
She climbed up and went home.

Freja Speedie (12)
Antrim Grammar School, Antrim

Spiders

Stalking the alleys,
Climbing the walls,
They're silent and deadly,
Even if they fall.

Across the street
They scurry.
They're not just spiders,
They're tarantulas,
Big and furry!

Anna Wallace (12)
Antrim Grammar School, Antrim

Halloween Time

It's time, it's time,
It's Halloween time,
It's time to have fun
And it's time to be scared.

There's witches and wizards,
There's wands and cons,
There's bats and cats,
While wearing huge hats.

There's lots of spiders,
Big black ones too!
They're as scary as ever,
So watch your back.

On each doorstep
There's a pumpkin,
They're all orange with a bright light.
They have funny faces
Carved on their heads.

Rebecca Thompson (11)
Antrim Grammar School, Antrim

A Lot Of Homework And Some Poems

First lesson maths,
And what comes with maths?
A lot of homework!

Maths homework is . . .
Complete the textbook.
Yes, all five million pages!
Also, we need to learn our
Twenty-seven trillion times tables!
Can this day get any worse?

For English we need to write poems!
Poems - why poems?
All poems are . . .
Boring and not at all interesting!

We read some poems in class
And we all fall asleep!

David Porter (12)
Antrim Grammar School, Antrim

Night

It was a stormy night,
The children were asleep,
The animals were tired,
Especially the sheep.
Grazing all day,
Running away,
Being chased by the dog,
Finding shelter in a log.
But when night comes,
Even the sheepherding boys are done.

Paul Cosby (11)
Antrim Grammar School, Antrim

The Hurt Bird

The fresh air of a crisp spring morning,
The men from the gun club were out shooting birds.
They came around the corner in their cars,
Suddenly they braked really hard.
A bird was crossing the road.
It had hurt its leg.
They got out of their cars,
They stood there in admiration.
One of the men picked it up.
He put it in the back of his car,
He took it to the vet's.
The vet treated its leg.
They called it Lucky after it
Just missed being hit by a car.
Now it's running about the back garden
Like a mad goose.

Philip Thompson (11)
Antrim Grammar School, Antrim

Horses

Horses start the day with a neigh,
Even when the clouds are grey.
The clippety-clop of their hooves as they whizz by,
As if they're about to take off in the sky.
Hold on tight, we're going to jump,
Look no hands . . . and oh, *thump!*
We trot in a circle, we gallop uphill,
We come to the gate and then stand still.
Lying down in the hay,
Munching on oats after a long tiring day.

Emma Carville (11)
Antrim Grammar School, Antrim

The David Brown 880

Chug, chug, chug,
The David Brown struggles up Tannaghmore Hill,
Smoke galore billows out of the exhaust,
The windows rattle and vibrate.
Drip, drip, drip - there's an oil leak.

The struggle to turn the steering wheel
Of a 43-year-old monster,
The clang of the spanners and screws,
The endless repairs that are needed,
The once white and red paint has turned to rust.

It struggles to keep going after 43 years of service.

Aaron Stevenson (11)
Antrim Grammar School, Antrim

Winter

Freezing fingers
Wrapped up warm
Hot roast dinners with smells that linger
Scary thunder and lightning storms

Frosty mornings that make you shiver
Making snowmen in the snow
Some thoughts of Christmas that make you quiver
Giving food to lonely hobos

Sad trees with no leaves
Staring out the window at snow falling
Wishing you were in the Maldives
Family and friends always calling.

Hāf Bishop (12)
Antrim Grammar School, Antrim

The Piano

Every morning I wake up and see
A big black piano staring down at me.

I wish I could play it, really gracefully,
But when I try it's not as good as it could be.

I also try to play a tune,
But I bang so loud you could hear it on the moon.

I want to play like others can,
But if you heard me, you wouldn't be a fan.

That was quite a while ago,
Now I play the notes that are shown.

Naomi Clingen (11)
Antrim Grammar School, Antrim

New York

In New York there's plenty to see,
Including skyscrapers that are massive compared to me!
A haven for many as some would say,
You have to go there someday.
There's Gucci and Prada and shops galore,
It's the city that never sleeps, so you won't hear a snore!
On a summer's day it's the best place to be,
Especially when you live near the sea.
In New York there are beautiful sights,
When you've been there your memories will be nothing but delight.

Jayne Clarke (12)
Antrim Grammar School, Antrim

Halloween

Halloween is a time of fright,
Halloween scares you at night.

Halloween is a time of fun,
Where everyone goes run, run, run.

The spooky house looks really scary,
And inside is not so merry.

The fireworks light on Halloween night
And flying up in the air in such a flight.

With pumpkin pie
And the moon in the sky,

Everyone's trick or treating, or running about,
You don't have to shout to get your son out.

Now we must go to bed, so goodnight,
For in the morning no one will be alright.

Josh Caldwell (11)
Antrim Grammar School, Antrim

Me, My Lego

M um's sunroom is my world
I t's full of coloured bricks
T hey cover all the floor
C rammed up to the door
H eaps of them, piled high
E ach one a ship to fly
L ego is my world!

Mitchel Pearson (13)
Antrim Grammar School, Antrim

My Dog

Happiness as I bring my dog home,
Excitement as I give him his bone.
Laughing as I pick up the phone,
Peacefulness as I stroke him, us alone.

Sadness as he visits the vet,
Now he grows old, my dear pet.
Anger when he stays in his bed,
My beloved pet lies there dead.

Tearful as I see his empty bed,
Upset when I see the hole in the gate where he fled.

Tense as I bring my new dog home,
Relieved because now I am not alone.

Hannah Brown (12)
Antrim Grammar School, Antrim

Winter

All the trees have lost their leaves,
Leaving all the branches bare.
It is such a wondrous sight
That I could just stand and stare.
As the snowflakes begin to fall,
The picture is nearly complete.
The cold turns all the dew to frost,
Which crunches beneath my feet.
The February sun glints off the snow
And icicles begin to melt.
Winter has gone, and along with it,
All the cold we felt.

Jonathan Boyd (12)
Antrim Grammar School, Antrim

Music

I can hear it ringing in my ears,
It makes me so happy,
It almost brings tears.

Sometimes a violin playing a rich noise,
Or possibly some pop music making a loud *boom*.

Maybe the tempo is fast,
Maybe it's slow.
Maybe the dynamics are loud,
Maybe they're low.
Some notes are fast,
Some are slow.

One way or another,
Music makes me glow!

Emily Bowman (12)
Antrim Grammar School, Antrim

Maths Homework Poem

I've forgotten my maths homework!
Whatever shall I do?
I might get detention
If I don't learn two times two.
My teacher won't be happy
If I can't produce my homework.
She'll probably go batty
And give me extra work.

My mum won't be happy when I ask her to sign
That ugly, annoying, frustrating detention slip of mine!
And what if I'm suspended?
That won't be very nice.
But in the end my teacher said,
'You just have to do it twice.'

Caleb Allen (12)
Antrim Grammar School, Antrim

Haunted House

Snap! go the legs of the skeleton
Bang! goes the noise at the door
Wallop! goes the sound of the mirror falling
Whack! is the sound the paintings make
When they fall off the walls.
Screams from the room next to yours,
Yells from under the bed,
I think you should go and never come back
To the house beside the graves!

Kyle Bainbridge (11)
Antrim Grammar School, Antrim

Bears

I really like animals,
My favourite one is a bear.
I love the way they look so cuddly
And I love their fluffy hair.

Although some people think they are scary,
They are really very sweet,
And they will really love you
If you give them a treat.

I would really like one as a pet,
Although they might be very big,
At least it still would be better
Than a messy little pig.

Anna Nelson (11)
Antrim Grammar School, Antrim

The Huge Mouse

I live in a house
That has a huge mouse!
When people visit
They run and scream about.

It crawls in and out of my lovely spout,
It eats all my cheese
And even nibbles on the peas.
When it comes out it makes my sister shout!

It destroyed all my plants
And eats my sister's pants!
It scares my dog
And ate my frog.

It has a house in my lovely house,
It gets past all the traps,
I think it might rap!
So this little mouse must go.

It bit my brother's toe,
So we got a man
That chopped off the mouse's hand,
So we never saw that huge mouse again.

Jordan McKelvey (11)
Antrim Grammar School, Antrim

Rain

I make puddles, I make ponds,
Sometimes I even meet the swans.

I'm clear as the sky on a sunny day,
In Northern Ireland I don't go away.

Not many people like me,
But I suppose they can't fight me.

When I fall from the sky,
(Which by the way I have no idea why.)

When I get down there all I see
Is everyone looking out at me.

Cameron McClurg (11)
Antrim Grammar School, Antrim

Buzzy The Fly And The Big Race

On your marks,
Get set, fly.
Buzzy the fly shoots off,
Around the cake he goes,
So tempted to fly right in,
Closely followed by Juzzy, the fly.
Coming up to the chocolate fountain,
Oh no! There goes Juzzy into the fountain,
And there's Buzzy flying down the home straight,
And Buzzy has won!
And unfortunately Juzzy has died at the age of two,
His burial will be held next week
At the fly graveyard in Spider World.
Come at your own risk!

Dale Morrow (11)
Antrim Grammar School, Antrim

Daisy

My dog is called Daisy
She trips over her ears
She's always hyper
But sometimes lazy.

She's a basset hound puppy
She's got really big paws
She loves her bed
And she's cute and fluffy.

It's annoying when she bites my foot
Her best friend is a bichon frise called Alfie
She chases cats
Her favourite toy is a boot.

She's so adorable when she looks at me
With her droopy eyes and long ears
She's like a hot-water bottle
When she sits on my knee.

I love my puppy, Daisy!

Victoria McKay (12)
Antrim Grammar School, Antrim

Football

Football is great,
But it's a source of hate.
Violence and fights,
It's full of spite.
Teams are ashamed
Because they are blamed.
It should be fun
But it's all about the 'mun'.

Josh Kirkaldy (13)
Antrim Grammar School, Antrim

Football Feelings

A kick-off with laughter,
A wall of joy,
A goal of excitement,
Why did you injure that boy?

A block of sadness,
A miss did make me upset,
A tackle that hurt,
I'm lucky I didn't make a Power Paddy bet.

We won the game and I was happy,
The player was ugly and
The referee looked like a troll,
But at the end of the day,
I scored a goal.

Ryan Myles (12)
Antrim Grammar School, Antrim

Our World

All the people in the world,
There are quite a lot,
All live in different countries,
Some cold and some hot.

There are also animals
That live among us,
Some we know and some we don't,
Some really big and some we crush.

And then there are plants
That grow in our soil,
All different types,
But none grow foil.

Steven Woolley (12)
Antrim Grammar School, Antrim

The Months Of The Year

January starts the year off with high hopes
And expectations for a happy and successful year.

February, cold and dark, soon ends most of January's hopes,
Four layers of clothing to keep out the cold.

March, spring arrives and flowers reappear to brighten the mood,
Thoughts turn to light nights and family holidays.

April showers show that summer is still far away,
Hats and scarves seem here to stay.

May ushers in lighter nights and cricket matches on the
village green,
But only if the threatened rain stays away.

June, school ends and summer begins. Days out with Mum and Dad,
Ice cream, sandcastles and plenty of 'Are we there yet?'

July arrives and cases packed, for surely it's holiday time.
Where we go I don't care, but plenty of sun when we get there.

August arrives and we realise that summer is drawing to an end,
Pack in as much as we can before early to bed for school again.

September means new blazer and shoes, for back to school we go.
New teachers and friends before the lesson ends.

October means I've got one year older as my birthday arrives,
Winter coat and scarf again, when I wanted a PlayStation game.

November, light nights are now a distant memory, dark going to school and
dark coming out again.
Snow falls and I am glad I have my coat and scarf. Thanks Mum!

December, another year over and only Christmas to look
forward to,
Perhaps next year will be different. At least I got my
PlayStation game.

Stephen Watt (13)
Antrim Grammar School, Antrim

Aeroplanes

Some are great metal beasts
Others are light as a feather
Some shoot, some don't
Some sink, some float
Some fly like a heli-chopper
And some are most favoured by
Groups of island hoppers
Me, I love them all the same
The ones that shoot
The ones that don't
The ones that sink
The ones that float
And especially the ones like choppers
But only if they don't break down
Like useless party poppers.

Daniel Pattinson (12)
Antrim Grammar School, Antrim

Hooked On Facebook!

As you get off the bus,
Getting on Facebook is a must.
You must say hello to Mum,
And up the stairs you run.

You know you're addicted and that's okay,
That matter can wait for another day.

The world of cyber space
Can be a pretty scary place;
There's the people that are good
And the ones that are rude.
Not everyone you meet is so sweet,
As stranger danger is not just on the street.
People on Facebook can be fake,
So make sure you don't mistake.

And before you comment or post on their wall,
Always think, 'Would I say this in a public hall?'
Think twice,
And always be nice,
As you never know, you may have to pay the price!

Sophie Robinson (12)
Antrim Grammar School, Antrim

What Not To Do When Your Parents Are Away

She kissed each cheek and squeezed me tight,
Promised that Dad and she were only gone for one night;
'There's food in the cupboards,
Don't forget to change your clothes,
Be in bed for nine, love,
Don't pick your nose!'

'Trust me, I'll be fine. You can be such a bore!
Don't you remember, Mum?
We've been through all this before!'

A big grin spreads across my face as I hear the front door lock,
Tonight I won't be inside, all alone, staring at the clock.
I grab my mobile telephone and send messages to all my friends:
'Massive party at my house - all night long, there is no end!'

My classmates flood into the sitting room,
Smiling faces, glittery costumes all around,
I am overpowered by the stereo's pop-rock sounds.
People tuck into the fizzy drinks and sweets,
I have spotted some strange people I have yet to meet!

The neighbours are complaining,
This party's getting out of control!
So many dancing people,
How am I supposed to tell them to go?

When I come to face the mess next morning,
It's more than I can bear!
Mum's best china smashed to pieces
And feathers from the cushions everywhere!

I don't know how I shall explain
What happened while Mum and Dad were out,
Aliens took over and wrecked the place
And started roaming about?

I gulped aloud and began to sweat
As I heard Mum approach the door,
When she saw the place, I didn't think
She'd be so glad to see my anymore.
She marched right in and saw the mess
And her eyes filled with fear,

She let out a shriek and looked at me and yelled,
'My goodness, what happened in here?'

Kristen Sinclair (13)
Antrim Grammar School, Antrim

The Day That Changed Life

Walking in that field
On that glorious day,
I never could have imagined
How these things could have happened.

Lying in the long grass,
Having the time of our lives,
I never could have imagined
How these things could have happened.

Looking at the beautiful flowers,
Smiling, having fun,
I never could have imagined
How these things could have happened.

But on that awful day
My family were taken away
And through the cloud of dust
I could hear the painful screams.

Walking in that field
On that glorious day,
I never could have imagined
How these things could have happened.

Tara Woodside (12)
Antrim Grammar School, Antrim

War

There is a time when this war should have ended,
The feelings between the countries should have bended,
There comes a time when too much has been lost,
All at a stupid cost,
But that time has passed as guns still blast . . .

There's been people killed
And too much blood spilled,
But what do we get from it?
Dead bodies in a pit?
Those weapons kill,
They shouldn't bring thrill,
Think of the children left without fathers,
As at their funeral everyone gathers.
Think of the sons' mothers,
Who comfort one and other
Through this stressful time,
That their children are caught up in crime,
Living life through the aim of a gun
Really isn't fun,
So why do we lead a life
That's full of knife?
When we could all be at peace,
If only that gunfire would cease.

Kate Peden (12)
Antrim Grammar School, Antrim

Cupcakes

Oh how I love biting into that spongy goodness,
The sponge is so fluffy and delightful to eat,
The icing swirled on top,
With sprinkles and flowers,
It's so tempting to munch.

Many hundreds get baked every day,
Giving the world a wonderful smell,
Oh they are made with
Loving and tender care,
Making them oh so delicious.

Peeling back the wrapper of a cupcake
Is ever so exciting,
You can smell the bun,
Your taste buds scream with excitement.

Ooh how a little bundle of joy
Can make someone's day,
They light up children's faces,
Even more than when they play.

No one cannot like cupcakes,
They are just something you can't hate,
So scrummy in your tummy,
And giving your tummy some TLC.

Oh how I *love* cupcakes!

Emma Olliver (13)
Antrim Grammar School, Antrim

Please Go To School, Son

Please go to school, son,
Because I want you to get your work done.
Please go to school, son,
Because you're letting me have no fun.
Please go to school, son,
Because I don't want you
To get interested in guns.
Please go to school, son,
Because you're eating my homemade buns!

Jonathan Myles (12)
Antrim Grammar School, Antrim

Halloween Night!

Halloween night, trick or treat
Tiptoe, tiptoe up the dark street
Go ring the doorbell but be careful who you meet
Witches, goblins, skeletons too
I wonder which one will scare you?

Ducking for apples can be such fun
Come and see the fancy dress and see who's won
Look at the pumpkin and its wicked teeth
And look at the candlelight underneath
Halloween night the fireworks glow
Please be careful wherever you go!

Lauren Wilson (12)
Antrim Grammar School, Antrim

My Best Friend

She is awesome,
She is crazy,
She is so very cool,
She is mad
And slightly loopy,
She rocks! It's true,
Sometimes she drives me up the wall
And around the bend too!
But I love her to pieces
And without her I couldn't do!
My best friend is always there
To help me when I'm down,
And to make me smile!
She is my bezzie, my Biffle and my Boff,
That's . . . Bestie,
Best friend for life,
And my best friend forever.
I can be myself around her,
I make a fool of myself but she doesn't care.
She overlooks my little flaws,
Like a spot, or a bad hair day!
But helps fix the big ones.
I can tell her anything,
I'd trust her with my life,
I really would!
If I didn't have my bezzie,
I don't know what I'd do,
I'd be so bored and lonely,
'Cause she's so funny and loud!
My best friend is one of a kind
And very hard to describe,
But she is one of the best friends you could get
And I'm sure you're jealous 'cause you should be!
My best friend is the best
And I love her to pieces!

Victoria Clingen (12)
Antrim Grammar School, Antrim

Something That Matters To Me

My mum bought me him when I was seven,
I thought he was a gift from Heaven.

From the edge of his nose to the tip of his tail,
He's as white as clean, crisp snow, so pale.

The only thing that would make him stand out
Would be his pinkish-red eyes, on fire no doubt.

His tail looks just like cotton wool,
The sort that you just want to pull.

He grazes grass on a lead that my granda made,
He always likes to stay in the shade.

He likes it when the weather is blowy,
He is my rabbit and his name is Snowy.

Stephen Houston (13)
Antrim Grammar School, Antrim

My Sister And Brother

My sister's not just part of my family,
She's one of my closest friends.
She's there for me, no matter what,
I always turn to her when things go wrong.
The memories we have are irreplaceable,
And I wouldn't change her for the world.

My brother is very protective,
But he loves to wind me up.
He looks out for me
To make sure I'm alright
And when I need help,
He's there.
The laughs and memories we share,
I'll never forget.

Kimberley Fleming (14)
Antrim Grammar School, Antrim

It Really Is Not Fair!

I'm really annoyed with all the bankers,
Stealing all my cash.
In their swanky suits they earn a fortune,
Can't I get a bonus?

I need a mortgage to extend my business,
But the bank won't lend me one.
They aren't helping me by doing their job,
They really do frustrate me.

And the government aren't much better,
Sly and swanky too.
They raise taxes but we pay for faxes,
Why are they really cruel?

Yes, I know, there's hustle and bustle,
But that is no excuse.
Think about others just for once,
Get us out of this mess!

It's complicated, but now I realise
They aren't really that bad.
Their dictionary from shares to loans
Looks depressing and sad.

But why can they not just sort it out?
I still don't understand.
So now I have reached the true conclusion,
It really is not fair!

Ben Collister (12)
Antrim Grammar School, Antrim

Bedtime

As I walk up the stairs to bed,
These things start to swirl round in my head.
What will I dream about tonight?
Hopefully it won't give me a fright!

As I snuggle down under the covers,
I hope I won't have another
Scary nightmare tonight,
As soon as I turn out the light!

I close my eyes and drift off to sleep,
I wonder if I'll have a peep
Of the dream world this time,
With grass as green as lime?

Suddenly I'm in a dream
Where everything isn't as it seems.
It is wonderful and scary
And the monsters are quite hairy.

Then I start to run.
In my ears there is a hum.
Oh no! It's a wolf,
It's coming, I have to . . .

It's okay, it was just a dream,
I told you it wasn't as it seems!
I close my eyes to go back to sleep,
I wonder if I'll have a peep.

Rachel Cooke (12)
Antrim Grammar School, Antrim

Young **Writers**

The School Bully

Here she comes
Or should I say it?
She's the scariest thing on Earth
By just a bit
She's the school bully.

Her eyes are like knives
They'll cut you in two
That's why I don't look at her
And neither should you
She's the school bully.

After weeks of teasing
I've had enough!
I'll show her what for!
I'll show her I'm tough!

Kick, punch, smack!
Oh no! *Boooff!*
She hits me back.

The fighting goes on a little longer
But all of a sudden I start to ponder
Who's the school bully now?
I am.

Ann Allen (12)
Antrim Grammar School, Antrim

Not Again

Six o'clock, the news comes on,
Another town, another bomb.
I sit and wonder, *what is wrong
That this conflict must go on so long?*

Religious freedom's what we need,
If only everyone agreed.
Terrorists please pay heed,
Oh, not another tragic deed!

Please let this bomb be the last,
We don't want to hear another blast!
The years are flying in so fast,
But don't bring back our awful past!

I thought that this was over, done,
But then again, there's always one
That sees this as a form of fun.
I hate to think he's someone's son!

I think, *how cruel can you be
To kill an adult, child, baby?*
And with no reason that's clear to see,
You seem like a monster to me.

Your actions are unjustified,
To think that someone could have died.
How, in this, can you take pride?
And this is why I cried . . . and cried.

Emily Hunter (12)
Antrim Grammar School, Antrim

The Hockey Match

Getting into navy and yellow
Feeling tired but ready to bellow
Driving down the road
Nearly driving over a toad!

Finally here
Feeling a bit of fear
Warming up
But not cheering up.

There goes the whistle,
Ready, set, *go*
Running up the sideline wing.

Bang, in it goes
Cheers rise, spirits lifted
In it goes again, we're on a roll!

The ball moves fast around the pitch
Players chasing after it
Tackling to get control
Dribbling, passing
Success, another goal!

The whistle goes
The game is over
Now we're looking forward
To winning the next game!

Lucy Clarke (12)
Antrim Grammar School, Antrim

Poetry Matters - Northern Ireland

Clone Of Earth!

Discovery! Discovery!
Newspapers shout,
Don't you know what it's about?

Life forms grow, evolve and expand
In this new, forgotten land,
In the far distance, we can't see,
A new Earth? Alas, can it be?

Discovery! Discovery!
Newspapers shout,
I certainly know what it's all about!

Temperatures don't soar,
The sun? You'll want more!
But the sky, it's still blue,
How do scientists know? I have no clue!

Discovery! Discovery!
Newspapers shout!
Is it this they are all about?

Years of travel shall occur,
If you wish to see the new world, sure,
It's not that high a price to pay,
Though it's hundreds of years away!

Discovery! Discovery!
Newspapers shout!
Now we know what it's about!

Megan Hopkin (13)
Antrim Grammar School, Antrim

Unconditional Love

They're there through the good
And support you when times are hard.
We complain they care too much,
Maybe protect us a lot.
Truth is, they think it's not enough,
We're theirs to look after!
They've watched us grow up
And mature with time,
But to them we'll always be a child.
They warn us about the trauma ahead,
As they've been through it,
Like a personal guide book.
They do their best to provide as much as they can,
There's many ways
And many reasons why.
They love us, we love them,
From now till they're gone, they're ours . . .
Our mum and dad.

Abbie Hylands (14)
Antrim Grammar School, Antrim

Child Abuse

I hide the scars away from sight,
And the fear I feel every night,
When tears are falling from my eyes,
I feel sick and sore inside.
With all that has happened
I have lost my pride.

I've never had a happy mum,
She always seems to be so glum,
Then she comes home and takes it out on me,
If only Mum could really see
How much this has affected me.

The bruises all over my skin,
Scars on my body and within.
It seems to go on for so long,
And I feel like I don't belong.
But one day I know I'll be gone,
Away from this torture and fear,
Away from this horrible place right here.

Stephanie Houston (13)
Antrim Grammar School, Antrim

Losing Them

The darkness invades once again,
As I shut my eyes waiting for it to begin.
I can hear it coming, *snap, thud, bang.*
Thrills twist and trickle through my tummy.
I can feel them coming,
The soldiers on pursuit to attack.

I can feel the pain advancing,
You can tell everyone is hurting,
The loss of brave soldiers' lives,
The tears swell within their wives.
These people, their pain is inevitable,
These soldiers were forever unforgettable.

Closing your eyes becomes intolerable,
As those images flash before you.
The fact that they're gone is palpable.
You begin to lose everything that you argue.
You just keep going, fighting on,
Tackling everything, even though it's wrong.

The memories haunting,
Soon become extremely daunting.
You try to forget about them,
But you can never forget your men.
You can't sleep at night,
Nothing is ever right.

The pain becomes insufferable,
Until at last it's unbearable
And you no longer want to be alone.
You miss them at the gravestone.

Rachael Allen (13)
Antrim Grammar School, Antrim

Muffins

They can be cold, they can be hot,
Lots of different flavours.
They can be eaten with ice cream
Or a pack of Quavers.

They can be big or small,
In chocolate or vanilla.
You can eat them at home,
Or in your private villa.

You can eat them with friends
Or by yourself.
They can be freshly made
Or in a packet on a shelf.

Yes, they're muffins!

Cory Ponter (12)
Antrim Grammar School, Antrim

Bullying

Physical, cyber, verbal bullying,
I get them all the time.
Another day goes on at school,
The same old story . . .
'Ugly', 'Fatty', 'Loner',
That's what they say . . .
I try to go on
But it's too hard,
No one to talk to,
Nowhere to hide.
My world's falling apart
And it's not my fault.
There's no one who understands . . .

Megan Ferry (14)
Antrim Grammar School, Antrim

Money, Who Needs It?

The news it comes all doom and gloom,
The child benefit cut has come awful soon.
It's to do with me so I stop and listen,
Because there could be stuff I'll end up missing!
The people who cut it, it won't affect them,
In their mansions eating caviar and looking at their gems.
But this I know when my mum says to me,
'No, we can't go out and it's beans for tea!'

While they're driving their Porsche to The House of Fraser,
I'll be at Tescos spending a fiver.
No steak or salmon or champagne for me,
Just a meal for one and a cup of tea!
But are they happy? I ask myself,
While picking my beans from the very top shelf.
No cook for me or a butler at hand,
Just a microwave dinner and soup in a can.

The government thinks that it knows best,
And has better ideas than all the rest.
But why does no one stop me and say,
'What do you think? Let's do it your way!'
I feel so cross that they think they're in charge
When my mum's overdraft is getting very large.
I'll leave you with this very final thought,
What counts is who you are and not what you've bought!

Matthew Lenehan (13)
Antrim Grammar School, Antrim

Friendship

Friends, you can tell anything to,
To be there, help and care for you.
For cheering me up when I'm feeling blue
And just really for being you.

Someone on whom you'd depend,
That is a truly good friend.
Our friendship was so meant to be,
You're almost a part of me.

Whether the day is good or bad,
You're always there if I'm feeling happy or sad.
For all the time you and I spend,
I'm truly glad that I call you my friend!

Sophie Johnston (14)
Antrim Grammar School, Antrim

Children In Africa

Their clothes are old,
They fit them badly,
They have sad eyes,
It makes me worry,
They make me worry,
They have no shoes,
Their feet are bare,
They have no house,
It makes me sad,
I wonder what they eat,
It makes me wonder what to do.

Shannon Heaney (13)
Antrim Grammar School, Antrim

Hockey Warm-Up

As the warm-up starts,
Our nerves kick in,
Everyone is wondering,
Are we going to win?

As we talk to each other
About tactics and set pieces,
We are all wondering,
Are we going to be defeated?

When our chant is over
And we are raring to go,
We take our positions,
Waiting to go.

Now all that we are waiting for
Is that whistle to blow.

Kathryn Jones (14)
Antrim Grammar School, Antrim

My Guitar

My guitar has six strings,
It sounds amazing
When my fingers are blazing away,
Shredding metal all day.

From the main riff
To the side lick
The overdrive station gives
It that extra kick.

A distortion pedal makes
It sound weird and groovy
While the clear channel
Makes it play so sleek and smoothly.

Joshua Knight (14)
Antrim Grammar School, Antrim

Animal Testing

Trapped in cages,
Lonely and scared,
With so many other animals,
It's hard to be heard.

The footsteps are getting louder,
The whimpers have become a roar,
Everyone is screaming and jumping
For they know what is in store.

And before you know, it's over,
The pain is getting higher.
The burning sensation is growing,
You feel like you have been thrown in the fire.

And suddenly your eyes begin to close,
They are heavy because of the strain,
And you begin to wonder,
Will you ever open them again?

Sophie Hutchinson (14)
Antrim Grammar School, Antrim

Bobby

There are lots of thing that are important to me,
Too many to possibly list!
So I am going to talk about Bobby.
For those who don't know who Bobby is,
I'll give you some clues.
Bobby is smart and cute,
He is affectionate and loving,
He is always a very good listener,
He is alert and never misses a thing,
He is Man's best friend and he is also mine.
That's right, you've guessed it!
One of the most important things to me
Is my pet dog, Bobby!

Quintin Higginson (13)
Antrim Grammar School, Antrim

Rallying

I sit there waiting for the flag to lift,
I can feel the butterflies in my stomach,
And we're off.
As fast as I can,
I drive round the stage.

I start to feel the blood pumping,
Almost like an adrenaline rush.
I get round the first lap,
Now it's getting exciting.

I approach the final corner,
My heart's really pumping now.
Next thing I know, I'm over the finish line.
I breathe a sigh of relief,
A smile appears on my face
And I hear the words, 'Well done.'

Rebecca Kennedy (14)
Antrim Grammar School, Antrim

Dance

Exploding with passion,
The audience inhales.

Step by step then leap by leap
The attitude comes from the heart.

Like a swan the dancer is graceful,
But inside their head lies panic and fear.

Dance is not just a word,
But full of drama, art and passion for all to see.

As a dancer impresses onstage,
Each heart in the audience is touched and inspired.

On centre stage she pirouettes,
Round and round she goes.

The crowd is stunned,
But she's dizzy inside.

Dance is not just a hobby,
But a career, an act for all to experience.

Emily Gamble (13)
Antrim Grammar School, Antrim

Show Jumping

I pull myself up
Into the saddle,
Gather up the reins
And begin to warm up.

Canter into the arena,
Through the flags,
Up comes the first,
And clear it with ease.

The second, third and fourth
Soon follow,
Flying over each fence
With my heart in my mouth.

I turn to the double,
A tricky combination,
Jump them both,
Still safe and clear.

Turn round the corner,
Flying to the last,
A big leap over
And clear at last.

Abigayle Gill (13)
Antrim Grammar School, Antrim

Rugby

It's time, time for the fight
It is such an amazing sight
Each side giving their best
Hoping it won't turn into a mess

The whistle goes, it's on
But it isn't very long
Before you have fallen behind
By a try the other team managed to find

Then they score another and another
They are unstoppable
It's getting near half-time
The whistle goes

There goes the whistle again
It's the second half
Let's all get stuck in
We really must win

Soon he gets the ball
He is beating them all
But soon brought to a fall
'Ruck over,' the captain shouts

The ruck is there
Those players who dare
To jump right in without a care
We won the ball

We get the ball, score
And again and again
We are drawing
Until the last minute

The opposing team scores
The whistle goes
The match is over
All disappointed

We have given our best
So we sing and cheer
Although we lost
The spirit of the game will always be here.

Darren Glendinning (13)
Antrim Grammar School, Antrim

Hope

Another day beneath the surface,
In darkness.
The faint light from the torch,
To save power.
We don't know if we will be found.
33 men, trapped.
18 days ago, a rock fall,
We were trapped.
We hear a rumble in the distance,
A rumble,
A crack,
A humming,
Louder, louder and louder again.
Dust falls from the ceiling of our ceiling
And then . . .
A small hole appears on our ceiling,
And then light.
A narrow streak of light floods in,
As if from Heaven.
Hope.

Peter Mitchell (13)
Antrim Grammar School, Antrim

Loved Ones

I don't know why people die,
Especially the ones that you love.
Your granny, your grandpa,
Your mum or your dad,
Why do they die?
Who knows!
Maybe God wanted a special angel,
Maybe the clock had stopped,
Maybe your life had just come to an end
And that's it - *bang* - your heart stops!
Everyone thinks you won't see them again,
That's the end of their life,
But that might not be the way that it works.
Maybe they haven't left yet,
They might still be there, right there in your heart,
Where all the good memories are stored.
You will see them again someday.
Maybe tomorrow . . .
Who knows!

Chloe McMullan (14)
Antrim Grammar School, Antrim

A Shot In The Dark

I slowly push open the rusty old door,
Hoping its hinges won't let out a snore.
My finger tightens around the trigger,
I know that he is in here somewhere.

I take my first cautious step inside,
I stand still, lonely in the darkness,
Hearing the rain dance off the old metal roof,
My eyes scan the gloom of the interior.

I hear footsteps, no wait . . . do I?
Yes, I do, they are all around me now.
I back up against the wall and wait on my prey.

I fumble with numb fingers for the safety catch on the gun,
My ears pick up the sound of a traitor.
He is near now, I feel his presence.

I see the shadow of a one-time friend,
He jumps out, gripping a dagger.
I aim, close my eyes and let
A bullet loose from the chamber.

I hear the body slump to the ground,
Suddenly I feel dizzy and fall to my knees.
Opening my eyes I see it,

A flash of lightning illuminates for a moment,
A handle protruding from my ribs,

I feel queasy and faint on the floor . . .
The only sound to be heard is the dance of the rain.

Phil Magowan (13)
Antrim Grammar School, Antrim

Those Among Us!

As the day gets darker
And the moon shines bright,
They all begin to wake
On that cold winter night.
As you run from door to door,
Dressed up like scary things,
Like monsters and goblins,
And witches and ghosts,
They'll disguise themselves among you.
You wouldn't even know
If they pass,
Or if they stare.
But as the night goes on,
They'll enjoy their time of freedom,
Howling in the darkness
And giving you a scare.
But just before the sun comes out
To start a brand new day,
They all go into hiding,
Until they get their way.

Yasmin Mirza (14)
Antrim Grammar School, Antrim

It

I saw it again,
That thing from the other day,
That thing I thought looked strange,
It's back again today.

It looked a bit funny,
Like something out of the corner of your eyes,
Or like a word on the tip of your tongue,
I can't put my finger on it,
But it reminded me of someone.

Like someone I once knew,
But I have forgotten now.
Yes, someone I once knew,
But I forget now.

Jack Lennon (13)
Antrim Grammar School, Antrim

Optimism

Mr Optimistic
Always so happy
So full of joy
Never a sad boy
I wish I was in his world
Always positive, never negative.

Mr Optimistic
His sky is full of clouds
With silver linings
When his world is upside down
He can still spin it the right way up.

Mr Optimistic
I wish I was like you.

Karl McNeill (14)
Antrim Grammar School, Antrim

Rugby

R ough and dangerous
U nyielding on defence, never step back
G rind to a halt while a shoulder crashes into your side
B leeding head, bleeding lip, get 'em taped, stitched or stapled
Y ou're playing the best sports game ever created!

Matthew Braden (11)
Carrickfergus College, Carrickfergus

Fashion For Passion!

My passion
Is fashion
Blouses and skirts
Trousers and shirts

Spots and stripes
Scarves and tights
That is why fashion
Is such a passion

And that is my passion
For fashion or
My fashion
For passion!

Abby Adair (11)
Carrickfergus College, Carrickfergus

The Beach

I'm running across the sand as hot as fire.
I'm dry as a bone until . . . *splash!*
Now I am as wet as a sponge.
Then I go and eat my sandwiches,
The bread is as white as snow.
The sun is getting warmer
And beating down at me,
Now I am as warm as toast.
I hope to be as brown as a berry
But I'm still as pale as a ghost!

Tamera Nicholl (12)
Carrickfergus College, Carrickfergus

Summer!

Summer! I love the summer
With the sunny days.
A summer without a sun for me
Is like a beach without sand.
I cannot imagine my summer without having fun.
Wake up in the morning, put my swimming suit on
And go to the beach.
Having fun with my family on the beach,
Playing football and swimming,
And at the end of the day, remembering
All the fun and the good things I had done.
I love the summer!

Iúri Sousa (12)
Carrickfergus College, Carrickfergus

Sweeties

Sweets, *yum-yum*,
Tasty as can be,
Chocolate's delicious,
Nothing can beat it,
They're both so nice,
I eat loads of them with delight,
Chocolate and buns are my favourites,
Yummy, yum-yum,
But they're both so nice!

Sarah-Louise Boyd (11)
Carrickfergus College, Carrickfergus

The Chilean Miners

Those Chilean miners stuck down there
Really and truly so deep
Down in the dark they're all alone
Those 33 men all in a row

Life can be cruel in many ways
And sometimes things will go wrong
The families are worried and so are their friends
And we don't know what's going on down there

Life can be cruel in many ways
For those Chilean miners stuck down there.

Tom Scott (12)
Carrickfergus College, Carrickfergus

War

Through World War I
And World War II
All the weapons that
We have used,
All the bloodshed,
All the tears,
The greatest war of all
Is when the family hears
Stand by me
We will stop this war
And bring world peace
Once and for all.

Stephen Cookson (11)
Carrickfergus College, Carrickfergus

Snowflakes

Snowflakes, snowflakes
Dance all around.

Snowflakes, snowflakes
Touch the ground.

Snowflakes, snowflakes
In the air.

Snowflakes, snowflakes
Everywhere.

Tori Haughey (11)
Carrickfergus College, Carrickfergus

Christmas

Christmas is finally here
My family started to cheer!
We all got excited, no need to fear
Because we really love this time of year.

The turkey didn't come, so we got into a panic,
My mum got a little bit manic.
After a while my dad got a new one,
So it was time to have some fun.

Oh joy! It started to snow.
Dad and I had a snowball fight
And we got very cold and low,
But we enjoyed watching the snowballs in flight.

On Christmas Eve I got my first present,
It was pyjamas and they were very pleasant.
Now at last it's Christmas Day,
I have lots of gifts to open and play!

Owen Shearer (11)
Carrickfergus College, Carrickfergus

Rugby

R ugby is ruthless
U nderneath the ruck can be very scary
G ood bridge is vital
B ut big people are hard to clear
Y es, rugby is *ruthless!*

Peter Campbell (11)
Carrickfergus College, Carrickfergus

Halloween Poem

There is a haunted house,
We dare not go inside,
In it are ghosts and witches flying high.

Tonight it's Halloween,
There's a party going on inside.
The ghosts and witches are laughing,
'Come join the party,' they shout.

We do not go inside
The haunted house tonight,
In case the ghosts and witches
Make us their delight.

Kyle McGookin (12)
Carrickfergus College, Carrickfergus

Me And My Family

M e and my family are close
Y es, we love each other very much

F riends are important to me
A lthough my friends don't like tea
M y dad works as a postman
I love my mum's food from the pan
L ike glue, me and my family are stuck together
Y eah, my family will love me forever.

David Alexander (11)
Carrickfergus College, Carrickfergus

Faith

On a busy street there stood a man
He held a walking stick and a mic in his hand
The man looked very much like a teacher
Wait, this man was actually a preacher!
Along came some boys who were extremely bored
They weren't amused by the words of the Lord
They stole all of the old man's stuff
But the old man, he had had enough
He said, 'You may take my stuff and props,
But my faith, it never stops!'
The boys turned and came back in a hurry
Their eyes turned from black to blurry
They said, 'We are so sorry for what we have done,
How can we repay?'
The old man gave them each, the word for you today . . .

Sophie Mc'Clean (11)
Carrickfergus College, Carrickfergus

Dance

Ballet, jazz, ballroom and tap
Watch the girls' dresses flow
Twirling around and tapping your feet
With your partner on the dance floor

Cha-cha, rumba, salsa and jive
Quickstep and American smooth
Dancing around to the beat
With your partner on the dance floor

Tap your feet
To the beat
Have fun and feel free
With your partner on the dance floor.

Erin Gillies (12)
Carrickfergus College, Carrickfergus

Pets

Pets are fun
Silly, cool
Happy, lovely
Playful, funny
And love me

Pets are helpful
But are the
Same to me!

Dogs are loyal
To me
Because they
Don't run off on you
They love their
Owner and that's
Dogs for me.

Christopher Wootton (11)
Carrickfergus College, Carrickfergus

Hockey

Tip, tap and the ball's gone,
These hits are really strong,
The other team is coming at me like warriors,
While I'm just a little stick,
While they're running about with knee pads,
While I'm looking over at my wee dad,
He was standing cheering me,
While I ran full of glee,
My friend, who is a hoot,
Shouted, 'Just you shoot!'
So I took my eye off the ball,
Missed the goal and hit the wall.

Alex Ogilby (11)
Carrickfergus College, Carrickfergus

Best Friends, A Promise Not A Label

Memories last
Forever and never
Do they die,
True friends stay
Together and never
Say goodbye.

Natasha Millar (11)
Carrickfergus College, Carrickfergus

Food

Food, food, it's so good
I eat it when I'm in the mood.

Food, food, it's so great
I put it onto my plate.

Food, food, it's so nice
I eat things like curry and rice.

Food, food, it's so cool,
I eat things that make me drool.

Food, food, it's so fun
I once made an iced cream bun.

Kurtis Hamilton (12)
Carrickfergus College, Carrickfergus

Friends 'R' Special

My friends are always there for me,
Even when I'm down.
My friends are always there for me,
Even when I frown.
My friends, they mean a lot to me,
They make me very happy,
The way a little baby feels
When it gets a nice clean nappy.

Rachel Mathers (11)
Carrickfergus College, Carrickfergus

Football And Fruit

To be a footballer you need to eat
Plenty of fruit and veg.
You need to be out running every night,
About five hours of training every day.
And don't forget the fruit and veg
Like apples, lettuce, pears and peppers.
And you can't forget the ladies.

Scott Laughlin (11)
Carrickfergus College, Carrickfergus

RMS Titanic

I'm a young Belfast boy and I'm 16,
I'll be 17 on 14th April 1912.
It's March and the Titanic is already finished.
I work as a Marconi operator on the Titanic,
My name is Harold Bride and my co-worker, Jack Phillips.
So it's the 12th of April and I'm on duty.
Three ice warnings have been received,
But one intrigued me, from the steamship, Baltic.
It was a 'berg two days away.
I told Jack to give it to the captain, but he refused,
So I put it in my pocket.
Two days later, one of the lookout men was sick,
So I covered his post and Jack covered mine.
Fred Fleet and I stood watch at around half-past eleven.
Fred was shouting with panic,
There was an iceberg straight ahead.
I pulled out the note from my pocket
And the co-ordinates were exact.
I heard a screech so I ran to the Marconi room
And went on duty sending SOS messages
To every ship I could find.
It was chaos.
It seemed no time at all before Jack and I were in the water.
I swam away and eventually got into a boat.
The next day was my birthday, but I didn't feel like celebrating
As my best friend hadn't survived the ordeal.

Ethan Graham (11)
Carrickfergus College, Carrickfergus

Fun Things

What matters to me
Are things that are funny
Lots of sweets, but even more
Lots of money

I like movies, books
And lots of jokes
But I don't like it
When someone gloats

My computer, my Xbox
My DS and Wii
They're all the things
That matter to me.

Jordan Spence (11)
Carrickfergus College, Carrickfergus

Music

Music makes the world go round,
Some hear a noise, some hear a sound.
Music is a brilliant sound,
Though when some hear it they hit the ground.

It comes and goes,
Stays and flows,
Some even say it blows.

You know it's there
And will always be,
It means nothing to you,
But so much to me.

Sophie McFall (11)
Carrickfergus College, Carrickfergus

Phones

P eople can text you and ring you to check out what's happening
H appy times with your mobile
O n time when there is an alarm
N o one has the same outstanding music as me
E veryone should have a phone, they are the best thing ever.

Rhiannon McFadden (11)
Carrickfergus College, Carrickfergus

Family!

F amily is so freaky,
   they made my bath tap leaky!
A ll of them care about me,
   so much they give me lots of money.
M y family is the best,
   they always let me have a big, long rest.
I love my family so much,
   sometimes we have a big munch.
L ife is fun with my family,
   I love them too because they're funny.
Y ou like my poem? I hope you do,
   That's probably what it's like to live in a zoo.

Abby Wilson (10)
Carrickfergus College, Carrickfergus

Science, Science

Science; science is so great
Science; science, just don't be late
Science; science, so many gases
Science; science, wear safety glasses

Science; science, I am a learner
Science; science, I love Bunsen burners
Science; science, the flame is so hot
Science; science, it could burn you a lot.

James Sharples (11)
Carrickfergus College, Carrickfergus

Family

F amily is important to me, they really mean a lot to me
A lways giving me money
M e and all my family
I love them and they love me
L ove is all that we need
Y ou and me.

Dion Maguire (11)
Carrickfergus College, Carrickfergus

Four Important Things

Some of my family flee
When they see a bee
The first important thing to me
Is my family

My best friend has a den
He is willing to lend a pen
But he is my bestest friend
My second most important thing to me
Is a friend

I like runny honey
Sometimes I am very funny
But not as funny as Bugs Bunny
The third most important thing to me

I laugh that hard I fly high
Sometimes I want to fly
To make the time go by
I like to watch 'Family Guy'.

Kane Brennan (11)
Carrickfergus College, Carrickfergus

Poetry Matters - Northern Ireland

Football Is Cool

Football is cool
Football is fun
You can enjoy it out in the sun

You get the ball
You put it in the net
Now you're said to be the best player yet

Foot, football is cool
Football is fun
You can enjoy it out in the sun

You get the ball
You're tackled really hard
Now you're hurt
On the ground

Foot, football is cool
Football is fun
You can enjoy it out in the sun.

Owen MacLeod (12)
Carrickfergus College, Carrickfergus

Friend

F unny at all times
R ight there for you
I sn't something to lose
E ven at your darkest hour
N ever quits on you
D oes care.

Joshua Mitchell (11)
Carrickfergus College, Carrickfergus

Max And Brutus

M y dogs
A lways playful
X -rated because they are Rottweilers

B ig and soft
R ough and tough to each other
U nknown by strangers
T imid to us
U nconditional love
S hould never bite or attack someone.

Jordan Thompson (13)
Carrickfergus College, Carrickfergus

My Army

M any married people won't see each other for a while or forever
Y ou; would you be prepared to die for your country?

A ll the soldiers fight for their country
R emember those who lost their lives in all the wars
M any; there are many soldiers in different countries, fighting
Y ou; would you fight for your country?

Luke Fitzsimmons (13)
Carrickfergus College, Carrickfergus

The Somme

T he battle that shook British military
H ow men and women fought and died for their country
E verybody should know the history of this battle

S ome will tell the great story
O thers have died and fallen for us
M ore will fight for the British army
M ore we learn, the more we understand
E very year we commemorate the ones who died for us!

Kris Dines (14)
Carrickfergus College, Carrickfergus

Rugby

R ugby is a lot of fun
U nless you don't like playing in the scrum
G etting tackled and scoring tries
B rings smiles to everyone
Y ou must come and have some fun.

Andrew Campbell (13)
Carrickfergus College, Carrickfergus

To My Dad

Why did this happen, Dad?
I know that no answer will fit right.
I wish you could still be here, Dad,
I wish you didn't lose the fight.

It's like you die over and over.
Dad, it's like a tease,
A constant reminder of something I can't have,
I am begging you, please.

I don't know whether you
Are watching from Heaven above,
Maybe your soul is there,
But either way, I send you my love.

Kelly Brownlee (14)
Carrickfergus College, Carrickfergus

Friendships And Relationships!

Some are good, some are bad,
When they are over some may be glad.
With girls and boys
It will bring many joys,
That's the fun of a *friendship*.

One day they love you,
Next they hate you and you think, *what should I do?*
You will love them always,
You could even say they shine like the sun's rays!
That's the fun of a *relationship*.

They say they will be there, through thick and thin,
Though others would say *no,* now that's just a sin!
They vow they will never talk about you in unkind ways,
Next you find out they did the next day,
That's not a fun *friendship*.

But of course they aren't all bad,
They say they will love you and won't make you sad!
You say the same!
So next time think twice before you start to blame,
That's the fun of both a *friendship* and a *relationship!*

Jennifer Hood (13)
Carrickfergus College, Carrickfergus

I Miss You

I didn't get to say goodbye
I didn't think I would have to,
When I heard that you would die
I didn't want it to be true.

I just wanted to pick up the phone,
Just to talk before you left us.
I wish you weren't so alone,
But you didn't want any fuss.

The day I was told
That you just died,
It felt so cold
I just curled up and cried.

I just wanted to say
That I love you
And miss you every day,
I don't know what else to do

But say I miss you.

Julianne Bailey (14)
Carrickfergus College, Carrickfergus

Table Tennis

Table tennis matters to me
The *ping* and the *pong*, the bat and the ball
I love the sound of the bat and the ball
But even though I want to fall
I love it so much
It makes me crawl

Everybody clap their hands
Because table tennis is the best sport of all
Well, that's the table tennis poem.

Josh Mannis (12)
Carrickfergus College, Carrickfergus

Halloween

Bang! Bang! The sound of fireworks,
Halloween is coming up, maybe the best season of the year,
But if you're not careful, well I think you know.

Pets don't like them as well as you,
So keep them indoors, if you want them there in the morning.

If your firework doesn't go off, don't go back,
Just walk away, if you want to keep your fingers!

So be safe with your fireworks!

Jack White (12)
Carrickfergus College, Carrickfergus

Football Poem

I like football very much
I think it is great fun
The only time I don't like it
Is if we're losing 3-1

The crowd stand quietly at the side
Until a goal I score
The crowd goes wild
Jumps up and down and lets out an almighty roar

I love it when I slip and slide
From right to left I go
I kick the ball across the pitch
A perfect pass to Joe.

Ryan Jeavons (11)
Carrickfergus College, Carrickfergus

Acrostic

A n acrostic poem
C an be about anything
R eally
O f course, some people like to
S tart each line as a sentence
T hough
I prefer weaving words into a
C reation that's more free form.

Joshua Nicholson (13)
Carrickfergus College, Carrickfergus

Football Poem

Football is cool,
It is better than school.
I like my kit,
It makes me have a good hit.

Sometimes I get mucky
And I strike it lucky.
The keeper had no chance.
He was pants!

As the player studs my knee,
Where's the referee?
The referee finally gives a foul,
I hear the crowd howl and howl.

As our manager cheers,
The other team's manager is brought down in tears.
My manager is pleased,
And now my legs have seized.

Colter Binnie (11)
Carrickfergus College, Carrickfergus

My Life

What do I want from life?
Get a job, have a wife?
Too far away, I'm glad to say,
Need to play Xbox every day.

I love my family and my dog,
Walks with her are a jog.
Going out to play with my mates,
Through the fields and over the gates.

Christmas and holidays are so good,
And I love to eat freezer food,
Chicken and pizza, that's my lot,
I'm really happy with what I've got.

Niall Douglas (13)
Carrickfergus College, Carrickfergus

Rugby

R unning about with muck to my knee,
U niforms get dirty, it's the best way to be.
G ame's about to start, filled with anticipation,
B oys running around, thinking they play for the nation.
Y es! I scored a try, the other team want to cry.

Gareth Smith (13)
Carrickfergus College, Carrickfergus

Garbage

G rounds (coffee)
A pple (core)
R inds (melon)
B anana (peel)
A nchovies (from a pizza I wouldn't eat)
G rapes (too ripe to eat)
E mptying the stinking bag (my job).

Jonny Bingham (13)
Carrickfergus College, Carrickfergus

Autumn Time

The days grow shorter,
The winds get colder,
The leaves are rustling and bustling, burling around
And form a golden carpet on the ground.

The berries in the hedgerows
Are filled with ripeness, the birds feed.
The squirrels stash their hard-earned hoard
As they prepare their winter store.

Melissa Meldrum (13)
Carrickfergus College, Carrickfergus

Love

I can't get to sleep at night,
I pace in my head,
Thoughts of you deepen,
I can't get this feeling to go.
What is this feeling?
I think they call it love.

Kirstyn Ferris (14)
Carrickfergus College, Carrickfergus

Fire Blaze

F ire, fire blazing up, burning, breaking all my stuff
I n the building I hear all, 'Help!' they shout, but no one hears
R anting, raging, the fire shouts
E nchanted by the fire glow and sprout

B lock all the doors and exits
L ucky, lucky, all get out
A ll to live another day
Z ipped through, the fire did
E nding with a *bang,* the building fell.

Glenn McKee (13)
Carrickfergus College, Carrickfergus

Books

Books
A place to lose yourself
A place to be free

Gladly diving into a place unknown
Making friends, meeting lovers or
Forming a bond that can never be undone

Not knowing what's around the next corner
Until you're already there
A mystical tale, a gripping fantasy

A riveting romance, a great mystery
A devastating crime and deadly secrets
Gripping phrases to catch your attention

It doesn't matter what story
It doesn't matter when or where it's set
Wonderful stories to feed your imagination.

Shannon Craney (13)
Carrickfergus College, Carrickfergus

My Brother

My brother, I miss you.
Remember when we tried to play 'Guess Who?'
I'm glad we don't fight,
I'm amazed about your height.

My brother, I love you,
I hope you love me too.
I want to see you,
I remember the things you did,
Remember the notepads you hid.

I want you back,
I hope you will be in my Christmas sack.
Please come home,
You are not alone.

Rachel McVeigh (12)
Carrickfergus College, Carrickfergus

Friendship Poem

We met when we were three years old,
In a very large building that was so very cold.
I will always remember the time and the place,
I will always recall the look on your face.

We are always together and never apart,
I will always remember when our friendship did start.
We will always be friends through good and bad,
I will comfort you when you are so sad.

Every weekday morning we go to school,
In our shirts and blazers we feel very slick and cool.
When we come home, we get changed and play.
Sometimes at weekends I try to get an overnight stay.

I thank you for the joy you bring,
When we are walking in the park, we hear the birds sing.
I want to say you will always be in my heart,
And hope that we will never be apart!

Olivia Donaghy (11)
Carrickfergus College, Carrickfergus

What's Important To Me

One of the most important things is
Sitting in front of the telly
Surrounded by lots of things
With which to fill my belly.

My seat is nice and comfy
And the fire looks nice and cosy.
My mouth is full of Munchies
And my cheeks are getting rosy.

My brother is on the computer
So the TV remote's all mine
And mummy's not too bothered,
She's just drinking her wine.

I've got room to put my feet up
And my cat is on my knee.
Everybody's happy
And that's what's important to me.

Matthew Dyer (11)
Carrickfergus College, Carrickfergus

The Football Match

The players came out of the tunnel
Hoping to do us proud
I'm sure they were nervous
When they heard the cheering crowd

The reds were near the goal
And they scored
We leapt off our seats
No chance of getting bored

And then there was a corner
Our hearts were in our mouths
The referee wasn't happy
He made it into a foul

Half-time came and went
Here we go again
It wasn't as good this time
It was tiring for our men

The other team was stronger
They seemed to be gaining
And then our luck was in
It must have been the training

Our man scored with a header
The goalkeeper was too slow
They were disappointed
But it was a really good show

Their team collected their medals
While ours made their way up
It couldn't have ended better
As ours collected the cup.

Ross McGinnis (13)
Carrickfergus College, Carrickfergus

Dance!

As soon as you open the door
Nothing matters, all fears are gone
You walk across the room
Slip on your silk-ribbon shoes
And when you start you feel as light as a feather

The twists, the turns
The lifts, the falls
It's as though you have been sprinkled with fairy dust
You run, then jump
You feel like a bird taking off on a masterful journey

The energy falling over you
The thrill of knowing you're right where you want to be
Every move practised over and over again
No fault, it's now or never
As you leap out on to the stage you feel free

Faultless moves, endless spins
Tricky turns and lovely lifts
Everything is right, nothing can stop you
Up and down, twists and turns
It's done, it's finished

What matters to me?
What matters to you?
As you slip off the silk-ribbon shoes
As you walk out that magical door
All your fears are washed away.

Laura Webb (12)
Carrickfergus Grammar School, Carrickfergus

War

War is like a pain that never goes away.
War is what brings friends to enemies.
War is the wrong of the world.
War separates the good from the bad,
But sometimes war is the only option.

War causes tears and losses in families.
War brings enemies closer.
War ruins homes and kills hope,
But sometimes war can cause peace.
War cannot be stopped.

Jamie Ross (12)
Carrickfergus Grammar School, Carrickfergus

What Matters To Me

Friends And Family

Family is like a blanket when you're cold,
Around you when you need it most.

Friends are there for you,
For telling your deepest, darkest secrets to.

If we didn't have friends and family,
We would sink into our own dark world.

Music

Music sweeps you away,
Each and every day.

Whether it's jazz or pop,
Even hip hop,
We need music.

Emily Wilson (11)
Carrickfergus Grammar School, Carrickfergus

What Is Love?

Love is about your heart swelling into a giant balloon,
Love is when you get that electric feeling inside
When you look at him,
Love is that eternal, everlasting power
That makes your bones shiver.

Love is when you think about him all night,
Love is when your mind explodes,
Love is when your heart breaks
And he picks up the pieces.
Really, love is love and that will never change.

Charlotte Majury (12)
Carrickfergus Grammar School, Carrickfergus

Friends And Family

Laughter, playing
Love, sharing
Looking out for one another.

Caring, baking
Reading, writing
Christmas cards and gifts.

Comforting, giggling
Smiling, confiding
Secrets never let out.

Laughter, playing
Love, sharing
Family and friends together.

Clara Rose Armstrong (11)
Carrickfergus Grammar School, Carrickfergus

What Matters To Me?

I ndicating, for the next instrument to play
N odding to the sound of the instruments
S ound travelling out from the basses
T ambourine, a part of the drum kit to keep in time
R ound sounds coming from the flutes
U nderstanding the sound of the parts together
M arkings, the dynamics, time changes, rifts and ralls
E nding the piece together in time
N odding to the players telling them to get ready to play
T ogether the instruments make beautiful music.

Aoife Burgess (11)
Carrickfergus Grammar School, Carrickfergus

My Family

M y family loves me, no matter what I do
Y ells at me if I do something really wrong

F amily is a very nice thing to have when your friends aren't there
A lways there for me, no matter what I wear
M y family shares everything with me like love, friendship and care
I ncredibly kind to me whether I'm good or bad
L ots of love and comfort towards me, even if I'm mad
Y et even if I hate them, I know I'm not alone.

Kate McConnell (13)
Carrickfergus Grammar School, Carrickfergus

Missing You

Today I thought of you
Even more than usual.
It's been three years,
I couldn't believe it.
I miss all your hugs and kisses,
But most of all,
Just you!

Today I thought of you
And couldn't help but cry.
I miss you so much,
Now there is an empty space in my heart
Just waiting to be filled but
I don't think it ever will; now it's . . .
Just me!

Today I thought of you,
I remembered all the good times,
It brought a fun-filled smile to my face;
The beach - when I fell you picked me up,
The bath - I closed my eyes but you were
Still there; those times it was . . .
Just us!

Megan O'Callaghan (13)
Carrickfergus Grammar School, Carrickfergus

Featured Poets:
DEAD POETS
AKA Mark Grist & MC Mixy

Mark Grist and MC Mixy joined forces to become the 'Dead Poets' in 2008.

Since then Mark and Mixy have been challenging the preconceptions of poetry and hip hop across the country. As 'Dead Poets', they have performed in venues ranging from nightclubs to secondary schools; from festivals to formal dinners. They've appeared on Radio 6 Live with Steve Merchant, they've been on a national tour with Phrased and Confused and debuted their show at the 2010 Edinburgh Fringe, which was a huge success.

Both Mark and Mixy work on solo projects as well as working together as the 'Dead Poets'. Both have been Peterborough's Poet Laureate, with Mixy holding the title for 2010.

The 'Dead Poets' are available for workshops in your school as well as other events. Visit www.deadpoetry.co.uk for further information and to contact the guys!

Read on to pick up some fab writing tips!

Your WORKSHOPS

In these workshops we are going to look at writing styles and examine some literary techniques that the 'Dead Poets' use. Grab a pen, and let's go!

Rhythm Workshop

Rhythm in writing is like the beat in music. Rhythm is when certain words are produced more forcefully than others, and may be held for longer duration. The repetition of a pattern is what produces a 'rhythmic effect'. The word rhythm comes from the Greek meaning of 'measured motion'.

Count the number of syllables in your name. Then count the number of syllables in the following line, which you write in your notepad: 'My horse, my horse, will not eat grass'.

Now, highlight the longer sounding syllables and then the shorter sounding syllables in a different colour.

Di dum, di dum, di dum, di dum is a good way of summing this up.

You should then try to write your own lines that match this rhythm. You have one minute to see how many you can write!

Examples include:
'My cheese smells bad because it's hot'
and
'I do not like to write in rhyme'.

For your poem, why don't you try to play with the rhythm? Use only longer beats or shorter beats? Create your own beat and write your lines to this?

Did you know ... ?

Did you know that paper was invented in China around 105AD by Ts'ai Lun. The first English paper mill didn't open until 1590 and was in Dartford.

Rhyme Workshop

Start off with the phrase 'I'd rather be silver than gold' in your notepad. and see if you can come up with lines that rhyme with it -
'I'd rather have hair than be bald'
'I'd rather be young than be old'
'I'd rather be hot than cold'
'I'd rather be bought than sold'

Also, pick one of these words and see how many rhymes you can find:

Rose

Wall

Warm

Danger

What kinds of rhymes did you come up with? Are there differences in rhymes? Do some words rhyme more cleanly than others? Which do you prefer and why?

Lists Workshop

Game - you (and you can ask your friends or family too) to write as many reasons as possible for the following topics:

Annoying things about siblings

The worst pets ever

The most disgusting ingredients for a soup you can think of

Why not try writing a poem with the same first 2, 3 or 4 words?

I am ...

Or

I love it when ...

Eg:

I am a brother

I am a listener

I am a collector of secrets

I am a messer of bedrooms.

Onomatopoeia Workshop

Divide a sheet of A4 paper into 8 squares.

You then have thirty seconds to draw/write what could make the following sounds:

Splash	Ping
Drip	Bang
Rip	Croak
Crack	Splash

Now try writing your own ideas of onomatopoeia. Why might a writer include onomatopoeia in their writing?

Repetition Workshop

Come up with a list of words/phrases, aim for at least 5. You now must include one of these words in your piece at least 6 times. You aren't allowed to place these words/phrases at the beginning of any of the lines.

Suggested words/phrases:

Why

Freedom

Laughing

That was the best day ever

I can't find the door

I'm in trouble again

The best

Workshop
POETRY 101

Below is a poem written especially for poetry matters, by MC Mixy. Why not try and write some more poems of your own?

What is Matter?
© MC Mixy

What matters to me may not be the same things that matter to you
You may not agree with my opinion mentality or attitude
The order in which I line up my priorities to move
Choose to include my view and do what I do due to my mood
And state of mind
I make the time to place the lines on stacks of paper and binds
Concentrate on my artwork hard I can't just pass and scrape behind
Always keep close mates of mine that make things right
And even those who can't … just cos I love the way they can try
What matters to me is doing things the right way
It's tough this game of life we play what we think might stray from what others might say
In this world of individuality we all wanna bring originality
Live life and drift through casually but the vicious reality is
Creativity is unique
Opinions will always differ but if you figure you know the truth, speak
So many things matter to me depending on how tragically deep you wanna go
I know I need to defy gravity on this balance beam
As I laugh and breathe draft and read map the scene practise piece smash the beat and graphic release
Visual and vocal it's a standard procedure
Have to believe and don't bite the hand when it feeds ya

If you wanna be a leader you need to stay out of the pen where the sheep are
The things that matter to me are
My art and my friends
That will stay from the start to the end
People will do things you find hard to amend
Expect the attacks and prepare you gotta be smart to defend
I put my whole heart in the blend the mass is halved yet again
I'm marked by my pen a big fish fighting sharks of men
In a small pond
Dodging harpoons and nets hooks and predators tryna dismember ya
I won't let them I won't get disheartened I can fend for myself
As long as I'm doing what's important
I'm my mind where I'm supported is a just cause to be supporting
In these appalling hard times I often find myself falling when
Only two aspects of my life keep me sane and allow me to stand tall again
Out of all of them two is a small number
It's a reminder I remind ya to hold necessity and let luxury fall under
Try to avoid letting depression seep through
Take the lesson we actually need a lot less than we think we do
So what matters to you?
They may be similar to things that matter to me
I'm actually lacking the need of things I feel would help me to succeed
Though I like to keep it simple, I wanna love, I wanna breed
I'm one of many individuals in this world where importance fluctuates and varies
Things that matter will come and go
But the ones that stay for long enough must be worth keeping close
If you're not sure now don't watch it you'll know when you need to know
Me, I think I know now … yet I feel and fear I don't.

Turn overleaf for a poem by Mark Grist and some fantastic hints and tips!

Workshop
POETRY 101

What Tie Should I Wear Today?
© Mark Grist

I wish I had a tie that was suave and silk and slick,
One with flair, that's debonair and would enchant with just one flick,
Yeah, I'd like that ... a tie that's hypnotizing,
I'd be very restrained and avoid womanising,
But all the lady teachers would still say 'Mr Grist your tie's so charming!'
As I cruise into their classrooms with it striking and disarming.
At parents' evenings my tie's charm would suffice,
In getting mums to whisper as they leave 'Your English teacher seems nice!'

Or maybe an evil-looking tie - one that's the business,
Where students will go 'Watch out! Mr Grist is
on the prowl with that evil tie.'
The one that cornered Josh and then ripped out his eye.
Yeah no one ever whispers, no one ever sniggers,
Or my tie would rear up and you'd wet your knickers.
Maybe one girl just hasn't heard the warning,
Cos she overslept and turned up late to school that morning,
And so I'd catch her in my lesson yawning ... oh dear.
I'd try to calm it down, but this tie's got bad ideas.
It'd size the girl up and then just as she fears,
Dive in like a serpent snapping at her ears.
There'd be a scream, some blood and lots and lots of tears,
And she wouldn't be able to yawn again for years.

Or maybe ... a tie that everyone agrees is mighty fine
And people travel from miles around to gawp at the design
I'd like that ... a tie that pushes the boundaries of tieware right up to the limit
It'd make emos wipe their tears away while chavs say 'It's wicked innit?'
and footy lads would stop me with 'I'd wear that if I ever won the cup.'
And I'd walk through Peterborough to slapped backs, high fives, thumbs up
While monosyllabic teenagers would just stand there going 'Yup.'

I don't know. I'd never be sure which of the three to try
As any decision between them would always end a tie.

Tips and Advice for PERFORMING Your Poem

So you've written your poem, now how about performing it. Whether you read your poem for the first time in front of your class, school or strangers at an open mic event or poetry slam, these tips will help you make the best of your performance.

Breathe and try to relax.

Every poet that reads in front of people for the first time feels a bit nervous, when you're there you are in charge and nothing serious can go wrong.

People at poetry slams or readings are there to support the poets. They really are!

If you can learn your poem off by heart that is brilliant, however having a piece of paper or notebook with your work in is fine, though try not to hide behind these.

It's better to get some eye contact with the audience.
If you're nervous find a friendly face to focus on.

Try to read slowly and clearly and enjoy your time in the spotlight.

Don't rush up to the microphone, make sure it's at the right height for you and if you need it adjusted ask one of the team around you.

Before you start, stand up as straight as you can and get your body as comfortable as you can and remember to hold your head up.

The microphone can only amplify what what's spoken into it; if you're very loud you might end up deafening people and if you only whisper or stand too far away you won't be heard.

When you say something before your poem, whether that's hello or just the title of your poem, try and have a listen to how loud you sound. If you're too quiet move closer to the microphone, if you're too loud move back a bit.

Remember to breathe! Don't try to say your poem so quickly you can't find time to catch your breath.

And finally, **enjoy!**

Poetry FACTS

Here are a selection of fascinating poetry facts!

No word in the English language rhymes with 'MONTH'.

William Shakespeare was born on 23rd April 1564 and died on 23rd April 1616.

The haiku is one of the shortest forms of poetic writing.
Originating in Japan, a haiku poem is only seventeen syllables, typically broken down into three lines of five, seven and five syllables respectively.

The motto of the Globe Theatre was 'totus mundus agit histrionem' (the whole world is a playhouse).

The Children's Laureate award was an idea by Ted Hughes and Michael Morpurgo.

The 25th January each year is Burns' Night, an occasion in honour of Scotland's national poet Robert Burns.

Spike Milligan's 'On the Ning Nang Nong' was voted the UK's favourite comic poem in 1998.

Did you know *onomatopoeia* means the word you use sounds like the word you are describing – like the rain *pitter-patters* or the snow *crunches* under my foot.

'Go' is the shortest complete sentence in the English language.

Did you know rhymes were used in olden days to help people remember the news? Ring-o'-roses is about the Plague!

The Nursery Rhyme 'Old King Cole' is based on a real king and a real historical event. King Cole is supposed to have been an actual monarch of Britain who ruled around 200 A.D.

Edward Lear popularised the limerick with his poem 'The Owl and the Pussy-Cat'.

Lewis Carroll's poem 'The Jabberwocky' is written in nonsense style.

POEM – noun

1. a composition in verse, esp. one that is characterized by a highly developed artistic form and by the use of heightened language and rhythm to express an intensely imaginative interpretation of the subject.

Poetry TIPS

We have compiled some helpful tips for you budding poets...

In order to write poetry, read lots of poetry!

Keep a notebook with you at all times so you can write whenever (and wherever) inspiration strikes.

Every line of a poem should be important to the poem and interesting to read. A poem with only 3 great lines should be 3 lines long.

Use an online rhyming dictionary to improve your vocabulary.

Use free workshops and help sheets to learn new poetry styles.

Experiment with visual patterns - does your written poetry create a good pattern on the page?

Try to create pictures in the reader's mind - aim to fire the imagination.

Develop your voice. Become comfortable with how you write.

Listen to criticism, and try to learn from it, but don't live or die by it.

Say what you want to say, let the reader decide what it means.

Notice what makes other's poetry memorable. Capture it, mix it up and make it your own. (Don't copy other's work word for word!)

Go wild. Be funny. Be serious. Be whatever you want!

Grab hold of something you feel - anything you feel - and write it.

The more you write, the more you develop. Write poetry often.

Use your imagination, your own way of seeing.

Feel free to write a bad poem, it will develop your 'voice'.

Did you know ...?

'The Epic of Gilgamesh' was written thousands of years ago in Mesopotamia and is the oldest poem on record.

Wordsmith

The *premier* magazine for creative young people

A platform for your imagination and creativity. Showcase your ideas and have your say. Welcome to a place where like-minded young people express their personalities and individuality knows no limits.

For further information visit **www.youngwriters.co.uk**.

A peek into Wordsmith world ...

Poetry and Short Stories
We feature both themed and non-themed work every issue. Previous themes have included; dreams and aspirations, superhero stories and ghostly tales.

Next Generation Author
This section devotes two whole pages to one of our readers' work. The perfect place to showcase a selection of your poems, stories or both!

Guest Author Features & Workshops
Interesting and informative tutorials on different styles of poetry and creative writing. Famous authors and illustrators share their advice with us on how to create gripping stories and magical picturebooks. Novelists like Michael Morpurgo and Celia Rees go under the spotlight to answer our questions.

The fun doesn't stop there ...
Every issue we tell you what events are coming up across the country. We keep you up to date with the latest film and book releases and we feature some yummy recipes to help feed the brain and get the creative juices flowing.

So with all this and more, Wordsmith is *the* magazine to be reading.

If you are too young for Wordsmith magazine or have a younger friend who enjoys creative writing, then check out Scribbler!. Scribbler! is for 7-11 year-olds and is jam-packed full of brilliant features, young writers' work, competitions and interviews too. For further information check out **www.youngwriters.co.uk** or ask an adult to call us on (01733) 890066.

To get an adult to subscribe to either magazine for you, ask them to visit the website or give us a call.

Poetry Matters

What matters to you doesn't matter to me
What matters to me doesn't matter to you
I may like dogs
You may like cats
I may like English
You may like maths
But we can still be friends
What matters to you may not matter to me
What matters to me may not matter to you
But what matters to both of us is poetry
Poetry matters!

Ben Roddy (14)
Methodist College, Belfast

Halloween

Halloween is so fun,
Let me see the money I won.
Scary faces I see going to my door
Saying, 'Trick or treat?
Trick or treat?'
Fireworks in the air going *boom, boom,*
Like bangers, *boo,* and rockets, *ahh!*
I see people's faces, they're scary,
They could really scare you!

Jake McCullough (12)
Monkstown Community School, Newtownabbey

Winter - Seasons

A cold, wintry day,
Too lazy to get out of bed in the morning, usually.
I think I should make a move now.
Kicking the blanket out of my way,
Rubbing my eyes and setting foot on the floor,
Knowing that no one was home,
I screamed with excitement.
A thought came to my mind,
Why don't I sneak away to my friend's house?
Realising that I was still 'Miss Lazy'
I'd rather leave that idea.
Just as I was walking out of my bedroom
I received goosebumps.
When I was having my warm, steamy morning coffee,
I observed the snow falling; pure white.
Wearing lots of clothes, I stepped
Out of my house for a walk,
Entered a children's park,
Saw a boy playing.
As I was trying to make shapes from the clouds,
I heard a horrendous scream.
My heart beat faster as I raced to the spot
Where the ambulances landed.
Officers were blocking my way.
Confused in the cold, I returned to my house.
Lighting the fire, I continued my day as usual.

Seliya Varghese (13)
Monkstown Community School, Newtownabbey

Halloween

Colourful fireworks in the sky
Way, way, way up high
Sparkly decorations
And delicious sweets
Interesting costumes
With awesome masks

Haunted houses
With ghosts and goblins
People screaming all around
Terrifying witches in the night
Big monsters in the dark

Little kids trick or treating
Money and sweets being given out
Beer and wine at the parties
People dancing and having fun
Wearing their interesting outfits
Until the morning comes.

Tylor Armstrong
Monkstown Community School, Newtownabbey

Halloween

Witches and ghouls,
Pumpkin drools,
Bats, spiders and wolves.
Darkness and full moon,
Ghosts will arrive soon,
It's Halloween time.

Dunking apples and trick or treats,
Costumes all about the street,
Fireworks and sparkles in the sky,
Children scream as I walk by.
I am back from the dead
But just for tonight,
For it's Halloween time,
Enjoy the *fright!*

Zara Tobin (11)
Monkstown Community School, Newtownabbey

Death

I shed a tear once again
When I saw a picture of them.
I felt alone in the dark,
When I heard my dog bark.
When they died I felt useless,
Then I felt really clueless.

What happened that day
Up to this year
That day is all a blur to me.
I felt so sad
And really mad,
I couldn't stop crying.

Taylor McGookin
Monkstown Community School, Newtownabbey

Halloween

Fireworks are bright
Kids with fright
Party till noon
With party balloons
I saw a spider
That was close to the cider

It's dressing-up time
Can I have lime?
We're running out of time
We need to buy wine

Skeletons and ghosts and ghouls
Grinning goblins fighting duels
Werewolves rising from their tombs
Witches on their magic brooms.

James Wilson
Monkstown Community School, Newtownabbey

Halloween

Halloween, night-time for sweets,
A bucket-load of yummy treats.
Witches and werewolves, wizards' spells,
Vampires stink of horrible smells.
Trick or treaters at your door,
How fun it is to see them there,
It really is no bore.
Fireworks that *bang!* this, and *bang!* that,
It's enough to scare a bat.
Black cats and rooting rats,
Halloween night is every child's delight.

James McClenaghan (12)
Monkstown Community School, Newtownabbey

Halloween

Halloween is dark and everyone has pumpkins and fireworks.
All the kids have sparklers, everyone has Halloween parties,
Fireworks exploding in the air everywhere,
And the bright night sky filled with colours everywhere.
The music is always on all night,
Everyone is staying up all night.
Everyone dressed up and there are
Fancy dress parties in nearly every house.
Trick or treaters at your door all night,
All the girls are dressed liked witches,
All the boys dressed as zombies,
With their little trick or treat buckets filled to the rim.
Everyone loves Halloween because
It's just the time of the year when you get
Lots of sweets and get to have sparklers.

Jack Crowe (12)
Monkstown Community School, Newtownabbey

My Christmas Poem

C is for the Christ, child born upon this day
H is for holly to make our mantle gay
R is for red ribbon to wrap parcels with
I is for icicles on this cold winter night
S is for snow falling from the night sky
T is for turkey that is so good to eat
M is for manger where baby Jesus lay
A is for angels on that first Christmas Day
S is for stockings all loaded with toys

D is for dinner that everyone will eat
A is for antlers on every reindeer's head
Y is for that big yawn on that early Christmas morning.

Aaron Rea (13)
Monkstown Community School, Newtownabbey

Nature

Noisy animals in the forest
Chirping birds flying from tree to tree
As you move and animals move away
The sound of water splashing from the waterfall
The sound of water running down the stream
The rocks are spaced out in the river
The footpaths all over the forest
Lead you to different places
You and family can go for walks
And view all the sights
The forest floor is soft and crunchy with leaves
The sight of the tall, brown, mossy trees
And when your wellington boots hit the floor
The twigs are snapping.

Ross Watters (14)
Monkstown Community School, Newtownabbey

Summer

Children scream to get out of school,
Waiting to buy their brand new swimming pool.
It hits three o'clock and I'm out of school,
Woohoo, bring on summer.
As I'm out of school now and I'm in my car,
My mum says, 'Don't worry honey, it's not far.'

We pull up in our driveway, Mum gets out of the car
And screams, 'Oh no, we've lost our power!
Oh no, the tap's broken too,
Now we can't get in our swimming pool!'

It all ends well and that is that,
Because we get a brand new cat!

Sasha Tweedie
Monkstown Community School, Newtownabbey

Christmas Time!

The Christmas tree is full of decorations,
Lights are all over the windows and the tree,
All you hear is children talking about Santa
And what they want.
The doors are filled with Christmas cards,
Children behave and do everything they're told,
The children are all excited because
It's Christmas Eve and they can't wait
For the surprises they are going to get.
They think of all the money their
Mummy and Daddy have given to Santa,
And how expensive their presents have been.
They get lots of toys and teddies,
But most of them aren't played with.
You start to cook the dinner,
The lovely smell of the turkey
And the potatoes and vegetables,
Not to forget the dessert.
The children complain about sore teeth
Due to all the sweets and chocolate.
The phone has been going all day,
Thanking people for the lovely gifts they gave you.

Amy Gilbert
Monkstown Community School, Newtownabbey

My Pencil Case

My pencil case is full of things
Big and bulgy
With a picture on the side
A zip with the company name on it
Grey at the sides
Stitched with thread you cannot see

A box with 100 staples
And blue polka dots too
Bent to perfection
So, so sharp
I could inject someone with them
So, so shiny

My HB pencil
Yellow, black and red
Sharpened to prick a bully with
Completely pentagonal to get to grips with
But be careful not to lick the lead

My Bio pens
Hexagonal
Green, blue, black and green
Must watch out for my behaviour
Or red writing in the diary.

Matthew Bell
Monkstown Community School, Newtownabbey

Granda

It was a quick death, heart stopped working
It was a painful, emotional death

The death of the man
Who was like my second dad

The death of my granda
Just left one big, sad family

Suicide, yes I could do
Leave me in Heaven with him, yes it would

When I saw him he looked so cold
Then my blood went so cold

That's what it was like
When my granda died.

Scott Wallace (13)
Monkstown Community School, Newtownabbey

Halloween

H ollow pumpkins sitting on the cold doorstep glowing
A ll the spiders climbing up people's backs, going to bite them
L ate night movies of zombies killing
L ovely sweets sitting on the table, dying to be eaten
O range posters on people's front windows, staring at you
W itches flying in and out of streets, casting spells
E very firework going off with beautiful colours and noises
E nchanting parties lasting till early in the morning
N oisy children running about in the dark.

Luke Hope
Monkstown Community School, Newtownabbey

Christmas

I am snug with my family on Christmas Eve night
When all of a sudden I get a huge fright
Santa's reindeer's bells are ringing
While Christmas carollers are singing

My mum and dad told me to go straight to bed
But I stayed up all night instead
Full of excitement and joy
Hoping I would get my favourite toy

I look out my window to se the snow fall
I run downstairs and find the Sindy doll!
My brothers and sisters playing in the street
Making a snowman and it's so sweet

The snow is soft, the snow is so white
It's fluffy and delicate
Perfect for a snowball fight!

It's four in the morning, I just can't wait,
It's brilliant, exciting,
Christmas morning is just so inviting

The tree so big, bright and colourful
It's all just so wonderful
Presents big, presents small
I really love them all!

Meghan Hope (12)
Monkstown Community School, Newtownabbey

Christmas Poem

Presents, presents everywhere,
I can't wait to open but I won't share.
Wrapped with love in colourful paper,
I might sneak downstairs and take a peep.

Snow outside the window, beautiful white snow,
I can't wait to make snow angels.
Snow, snow, so frosty and cold,
I'll be playing in snow for twenty years.

Santa, Santa, I hope he comes soon,
When he does I'll be over the moon.
Cookies and milk on the fireplace,
When the reindeer see,
It will be a reindeer race.

Christmas tree, Christmas tree, so very new,
With tinsel and baubles green, yellow and blue.
Angel on top with her golden halo,
This is what happens at Christmas.

Nikita Bowers
Monkstown Community School, Newtownabbey

Seasons

Summer

Summer is fun and free
Summer is long and crazy
Summer is warm and exciting

Spring

Spring is bright and colourful
Spring is growing with life

Autumn

Autumn is cold and damp
Autumn is fun and colourful
Autumn is loud and spooky

Winter

Winter is wet and cosy
Winter is short and snowy
Winter is freezing and wet
Winter is fun and jolly.

Jasmin Younger (12)
Monkstown Community School, Newtownabbey

Nature

Nature, such beauty I see,
Incomparable perfection
Meets my eye with glee.
Views of forests, mysterious, alive,
Without all of this I just wouldn't survive.

At twilight I sit there admiring the stars,
Feeling the same way my dad does with cars.
I wonder sometimes who, and where, I would be,
If I wasn't, if I couldn't,
Forever be me.

The moon sits there in its place,
Putting a smile on the whole human race.
I have a rose, it's smell so mild,
But it looks so diverse, so wild.
I wish with the stars, I wish that might
Forever feel the way that I do tonight.

Shannan Vicary (12)
Monkstown Community School, Newtownabbey

Halloween

Fireworks are loud
Fireworks are colourful
Fireworks are wonderful
Fireworks are powerful
Fireworks are high

Monsters are scary
Monsters are ugly
Monsters are tall
Monsters are short

Trick or treating is fun
Trick or treating is scary
Trick or treating is quiet

Costumes are colourful
Costumes are scary
Costumes are nice
Costumes are dark

Witches are scary
Witches are bad
Witches are loud
Witches are mean.

Jake Peachey
Monkstown Community School, Newtownabbey

Seasons

Spring, lots of animals come out to play
Spring has lots of colourful flowers
Spring is warm and cuddly

Summer, what lovely days
Summer, school's off so let's play
Summer, so warm and fun
Summer, so thirsty and bright

Autumn, lots of leaves fall off the trees
Autumn, different colours everywhere
Autumn, starting to get cold so let's stay in and play
Autumn, so fun to play the Xbox 360

Winter, so cold and frosty
Winter, so windy and dark
Winter, so snowy and white
Winter, so dark so early.

Darren Downing (11)
Monkstown Community School, Newtownabbey

Halloween

Pumpkins are orange
Witches are green
Monsters are mean
Bats and wolves are together
Everyone is nice
But only for one night.

Fireworks high up in the sky
Some people are eating pie
Mums and dads are going out
So the kids show on their faces a *big* pout.

'Trick or treat?' I come to say
As I stand on the cold bay
Dunking apples is so fun
But I really want a bun
Ghosts will be coming soon
But I have to say goodnight.

Tammy Gourley (12)
Monkstown Community School, Newtownabbey

Poem

I will miss you so much,
All the years you were here,
But time will go by,
I will get through.
I will shed that tear
Every once in a while,
When I think of you it makes me smile.
I won't forget our memories,
Laughter, love and joy,
That I will keep close to my heart,
Where you will always remain.

Denika Cardwell (14)
Monkstown Community School, Newtownabbey

Spiders

Spiders at night,
Oh! What a fright!
Sitting on a wall,
Silent,
Watching and waiting,
Or crawling down your hall.
Creepy, crawly, skinny little legs.
Where did it go?
I have to know.
Is it under the mat?
Don't move your feet,
Not even one toe.
I see it now,
Uh-oh, uh-oh,
Where will it go?

Cillian McGoldrick (13)
St John's Business & Enterprise College, Dromore

The Winter

The winter is cold,
The trees move swiftly back and forth
dancing and enjoying the fun.

When winter comes the little squirrels,
hedgehogs and many more
gather up food to hibernate.
You hear them rustling in the leaves
as they run with fear.

When it snows we go out and play.
Family memories that will never fade.
The cold snow hits your face and you
get a thrill up your body like
jumping off a cliff into a
big pool of sea water.

The tree leaves fall gently with a gust of wind.
The trees are bare.
Children jump through piles upon piles
of yellow, crunchy, brown leaves.
Jumping, laughing, enjoying the day.

The day has dawned.
The children are snoring in their beds
looking forward to the day.
They're not aware that winter
will soon be over.
So have fun!

Kirby Mullan (13)
St John's Business & Enterprise College, Dromore

A Year On The Farm

The roar of the combine harvester
Whines in the distance
To the background noise of
The tractor as it rattles up and down the road.

In the field the harvester
Starts a new row.
The machine dies and drops a gear,
Goes into the heavy green grass
And the tractor trailing behind
Slowly makes its way up the bray
Clenching the clay as it slides
Gently downwards.

After the grass is in, the big slurry wheels
Are attached and the pipeline is reeled out.
The tractor comes trudging up the hill,
Then the lazy arm flips down
And pumps slurry into the tractor.

The ploughs
Are attached to the rear of the tractor.
The plough enters the soil and throws it up
Like rows of beech hedges.
Afterwards, the power harrow drops and
Whacks the clay into fine pieces.

Then the land leveller is attached
And the ground is levelled
And the sods are
Pulled to the side.
The last jobs are harrowing and sowing.
The grass, helped by fertilizer
And sometimes lime, starts to grow.

Dean O'Neill (14)
St John's Business & Enterprise College, Dromore

Nail Polish

I like nail polish,
It is so pretty.
It comes in lots of different cheery colours,
Gooey green, yelling yellow, blasting blue,
Popping pink and plenty more.
The cute little bottle looks up at you
Pleading to be opened.
Open it up,
Watch the polish daintily slip off the tiny brush,
Glossy, smooth and shiny.
When you put it on the tiny brush
It slowly glides across your fingernail.
While the brush spreads its bristles out
You can feel the cold nail polish on your smooth nail.
Nail by nail, stroke by stroke
I paint my nails.
Tiny bits might splash onto your fingertips,
But not to worry, quickly wipe them off.
There you go!
Now you have the nicest nails.

Eimear Curran (13)
St John's Business & Enterprise College, Dromore

My Sister, Clodagh

My sister lets nobody get in her way,
She has her own way for everything.

She is small for her age,
But she doesn't think so.

She is a giddy person and has a cheeky smile,
As if she was hiding something.

She enjoys school and every day
She comes home laughing
With the stories she has to say.

Clodagh loves all animals.
She loves going with Daddy
To feed the farm animals.
She is a daddy's girl.

Clodagh is creative and artistic.
Very active, she is never sitting
Around doing nothing.
We laugh a lot, we fight *a lot,*
Clodagh is funny and fun to be with.

Deirbhla McNulty (13)
St John's Business & Enterprise College, Dromore

Halloween

Ghosts and goblins and monsters too
They all jump out and scream, 'Boo!'

Black cats as dark as night
People in costumes give me a fright

If you yell and say hello
They say, 'Trick or treat? Now give me some, do'

I like Halloween, it is dark and scary
Monsters are all ugly and hairy

Witches, one broomstick
Bats with wings

People with sparklers
And shiny things.

Kayleigh Wilson (13)
St Louise's Comprehensive College, Belfast

What Matters To Me?

I like the name Megan because
Nearly everyone has it
It is a good name and it fits my habit
I like nature and everything green
I wonder what else could be seen?
Cats and dogs and everything else,
I like them a lot, and even myself!

Megan Magee (13)
St Louise's Comprehensive College, Belfast

Fashion

F un, funky, fresh, fashion
A nimal print, stripes, spots, straps
S hoes, heels, wedges, flats, boots
H ats, scarves, gloves, mittens, socks
I n store, on rails, on shelves, on you
O n your head, body, legs, feet
N ice, gorgeous, beautiful, lovely.

I love fashion!

Holly McGurnaghan (14)
St Louise's Comprehensive College, Belfast

Seaside Summer!

Dolphins in the sea, looking through the frosty water at me.
I lie on the shore thinking about all the things I could explore,
The underwater world all at my door,
Mermaids, fish and a whole lot more!
The sand between my toes and a butterfly landing on my nose
Are all the great things about the outside world.
Where to start, where to go? I don't know.
So many things I'd like to explore
And yet they're all at my own door.
The problem is I don't know how to swim in the sea
And to sit on the shore even scares me.
To see a mermaid so close and alive, or to touch a dolphin
Would make me smile, it would make me so happy and
So glad inside, it would leave me bursting with absolute pride.
To see all the fish and water animals in their glory,
Would make me happy and to all would be told the story.
So that's the story of my summer at the seaside all rolled into one
But to be truthful, you had to be there to experience the fun.

Nicole Millen (14)
St Louise's Comprehensive College, Belfast

My Family

I have a lovely family,
They are very important to me.
It consists of four people,
Mum, Dad, my brother and me.

My daddy is a special dad,
He loves me unconditionally
And when I was little he would
Bounce me up and down on his knee.

My mummy is a wonderful mum,
She loves me very much.
Even when life is tough,
She never gives up.

My brother is a monster,
He gives me such a fright,
But when he is scared and lonely,
I cuddle him at night.

I love my family dearly,
They mean the world to me,
Even though there's only my mum,
My dad, my brother and me.

Alisha Cully (13)
St Louise's Comprehensive College, Belfast

Real Love

Love imperfectly. Draw outside the lines.
Make mistakes, go crazy, don't follow
The rules, go beyond your wildest dreams!
Forget about everything, think untruly and
Laugh yourself silly, dance without shame,
Enjoy now!
Forget about the future and love madly like
You mean it, skip the drama and share
Endless thrills.
Stand out, be loud, never ever hold back,
Let your imagination take over, dream,
Hope to feel the happiness, feel the embarrassment,
Feel touched, feel anger, feel loved and wanted.
No limits, no rules, just love, it makes life worth
Living, fuel for the soul, a journey with no end.
Life is too short to worry, smile, be happy,
Be shameless, forget about everything.
Love, be silly. Don't make sense.
Life is so messy, so cherish it and
Don't ever look back!

Aideen Macauley (13)
St Louise's Comprehensive College, Belfast

Friends Matter

Friends matter
They really do
They care for you
If they are true
They share your life
Good times and bad
They're there when you're happy
And when you're sad.

Cara Mulhern (13)
St Louise's Comprehensive College, Belfast

What Matters To Me!

What matters to me
You're about to see . . .
I have a friendly feeing inside me.
My school is cool,
It matters to me.
I love my family, they love me too,
They matter to me!
My community matters to me,
It gives me an opportunity.
Everything matters to me
You see!

Caitlin Kelly (13)
St Louise's Comprehensive College, Belfast

What Is Important To Me

What is important to me, I've got to tell you now . . .
The loyalty of my dog, who I adore so much.
The name of this dog is Murphy Fitz!

Mumble Murphy, the love of my life,
The life that we live on the Donegal Road.
You want a Murphy, you've got a fluffy bear to hold.
It's him you want, not an old, scruffy thing.
A Murphy for everyone!

Laura Fitzsimmons (12)
St Louise's Comprehensive College, Belfast

Forbidden Love

Our love is like a growing vine,
It twists and turns through all of time.
We have our ups, we have our downs,
With our love we have no bounds.
I love your hair,
I love your smile,
With our love we could run a mile.
I really love you
And you love me,
But our love could never be.

Ciara Thompson (14)
St Louise's Comprehensive College, Belfast

Things That Are Important To Me

Living my life
And some day being a wife.
I live for the music
And hope to play 'Bad Romance' acoustically.
My computer matters to me.
What is important is getting my own house key.
Seeing my little niece in her communion dress,
Hoping she is the best.
But I don't need to hope
Because I know she will be better than the rest.

Siobhan Andrews (12)
St Louise's Comprehensive College, Belfast

Things That Matter To Me!

F is for my favourite website
A is for adding things onto my profile
C is for all the comments I make
E is for all the emails I get
B is for the brilliant games I play on it
O is for all the optional applications on the site
O is for opinions that can be made on people's photos
K is for all the kind friends I add.

Aoife McGuigan (12)
St Louise's Comprehensive College, Belfast

Scenic Walk

Walking along the uneven paths
I view the spectacular scenery ahead of me.
I ask myself, what could this be?
Because all I can see is the blinding sun,
It shone like a rebel diamond for all to see,
With the bright blue sky contrasting.
The gracious birds made their way to their next destination,
As if the clouds were a certain relation,
I stood in utter patience staring far afield,
The surroundings were a gift, in order to shield me.
I viewed the tall, mighty mountains,
As the wind gently rustled my hair.
I stood silently as my vision slowly came to a blur,
I witnessed the seashells hidden beneath the sand,
With the many detailed features that were held in my hand.
I felt the soft sand below my feet,
It triggered my thought that it resembled a golden, smooth sheet.
The sea swayed and it reflected my appearance,
The sun went down and the moon appeared.

Niamh Jeffreys (14)
St Louise's Comprehensive College, Belfast

What Matters To Me!

What matters to me!
I like to feel free,
Feel the wind on my face
When running a race
With my family.

My mummy, my brother,
My sister and me,
We love to race
Down by the sea.

We bring our binoculars
So that we can see all the wonderful things
Beyond the trees,
I love to feel free,
That's what matters to me!

Mandy McManus (13)
St Louise's Comprehensive College, Belfast

Christmas

Snowflakes falling to the ground,
Not a single noise around.
Children awaken from their beds,
Run downstairs with sleepy heads.
Screams and laughter fill the air,
Christmas wrapping everywhere.
Curtains open, Santa's gone;
All the parents start to yawn.
New clothes on, hair's all done,
The sky is grey, there is no sun.
Chicken's ready, vegetables too,
I love Christmas more than you.
Gloves and hats, nice and warm,
Outside a winter storm.
Make a man out of snow;
Moon and bright stars begin to glow.
Presents out, time to play,
I can't wait until the next Christmas Day.

Kerry Murray (13)
St Louise's Comprehensive College, Belfast

What Matters To Me

I have a family, Mum, Dad and brother,
I am dedicated to school, dance, acting and singing.
What matters to me you can tell by looking at me . . .
In school the one thing that matters to me is to have friends
And be kind, caring and loving to all around me.
The most important thing that matters to me in all my life now
Is success and to succeed in everything I need!
I go to Mass in my local parish and love to think and pray.
I also love wearing pink hairbands, necklaces
And laces on my shoes.
Look at how many things I have gone through with you.
Now you can see that everything matters to me . . .
It's all around me!

Sarah Mulholland (12)
St Louise's Comprehensive College, Belfast

Colours

Dark blue is the colour of the sea,
Green is the colour of a tiny little pea.
Yellow is the colour of the bright sun
And brown is the colour of a crispy bun.
Red is the colour of a clown's hair
And white is the colour of the fog in the air.
Orange is the colour of a butterfly
And light blue is the colour of the summer sky.
Purple is the colour of some grapes
And black is the colour of old video tapes.
Colours, colours everywhere,
It's so hard not to stop and stare.

Orlagh Headley (12)
St Mary's High School, Lurgan

New York

New York, New York,
A place that's big and not small
It's large and is welcoming, to a great deal of all.
The city lights will blind you as you stroll on by,
And the buildings are so tall you can barely see the sky.

Overlooking New York stands the Statue of Liberty tall,
Representing independence and freedom to all.
From street to street, yellow taxi cabs rush by
And overhead in Central Park, many birds are flying high.

New York, New York,
The city that never sleeps,
That's filled with joy and surprises on many different streets.

Shannon Creaney (12)
St Mary's High School, Lurgan

Autumn

As I look around I see no leaves as green as grass,
And we all drink hot chocolate right out of the glass.
I hear all the leaves crunch under the children's feet,
Also we start to sleep with a few extra sheets.
We all start to wear our scarves and hats,
And at Halloween, we all dress up as bats.
Everyone turns up their central heating
And it's that quiet you can hear your heart's beating.
All the animals go and hibernate
And nobody gets to stay out late.

Caitlin Cassidy (12)
St Mary's High School, Lurgan

My School

I go to St Mary's Junior High,
'Time for class,' the teachers all cry.
We go to form class in the morning,
At the desks the pupils are yawning.

The class works hard at the start of the day,
At break time we go out to play.
The bell rings for class to start,
We might have PE, or maths, or art.

Off we all rush to our next class,
We gather ourselves up off the grass.
Off we rush back in to the school,
I'm proud of it because it rules!

The lunch bell rings loudly at half-past twelve,
We stack our books up back on the shelves.
We go to the canteen, lunch is a blur,
We all give our tums some tender, loving care.

Our last few classes seem to last for ages,
Forever staring at black and white pages,
But we all know it's all for the best,
So we can get home and have some well deserved rest.

Amy Fitzpatrick (12)
St Mary's High School, Lurgan

My Little Red Kite

Up in the park with my little red kite
When it's up in the air, it's such a pretty little sight

It swoops and it sways in the bright blue sky
With not a care as the wind rushes by

I watch it fly up in the sky
And wonder how it will go so high

When it is blowy it flies away
Always ready to come back another day

I love my little red kite
It is always a pretty little sight

With all the colourful bows on the tail
It will never fail!

Really and truly I love my little red kite
It is such a pretty little sight.

Connie Callaghan (11)
St Mary's High School, Lurgan

I Don't Feel Well!

I don't feel well today!
I think I've got the flu!
The other kids go out to play
So I hope I give it to you!

My throat is very sore,
My head is now spinning,
There are tissues galore,
This bug keeps on winning!

My nose is very swollen,
My eyes are deep red,
I can't go bowling,
I'm still in this bed!

My temperature is sky high,
I feel cold and clammy,
My lips are almost dry,
I want my mammy!

Now I don't feel sad,
My temperature has gone down a bit,
I guess I'm just really glad
Now my brother has it!

Anna Conway (12)
St Mary's High School, Lurgan

Sight

Don't take it for granted,
Sight is what I mean
To see if things are light or dark,
Or yellow, pink or green.

There's a world of different colours,
Let's take, for example, blue.
The sea when it glimmers in moonlight
Or the morning sky I drew.

To see what it's like in January,
What it's like when the first snow falls,
The red and green of holly,
Or a newborn baby crawl.

To see a family holiday,
To see a big goodbye,
To see a brilliant picture,
To see a grown man cry.

So next time that you notice
A face that's full of glee,
Open your eyes and look,
You're lucky you can see.

Anna Daggett (11)
St Mary's High School, Lurgan

Summer

Looking up at the clear blue sky
I watch the birds fly up, up high.

Lying in the scorching weather,
My friends and I all laugh together.

Water fights and races,
We all dry our wet faces.

Going on wonderful trips
And on our way we have some chips.

Everyone's tired so they go in,
Waiting for another wonderful day to begin!

Hannah Abraham (11)
St Mary's High School, Lurgan

My Favourite Things

I have loads of things I like,
For example, flying a kite.
I like dogs,
I've got a picture of one beside logs!
I like cats, they're nice and fluffy
And sometimes they're puffy.
I like hamsters, they're really cute!
When I stand up I'm really tall
And they're really small!

Megan Grimes (11)
St Mary's High School, Lurgan

Homework

Mum and Dad say, 'Come downstairs,'
Just to make us sit on the chairs.

We have homework and we need it complete
Then we'll sit down and put up our feet.

I want to finish so I can watch the soaps
Maybe I'll even have a bowl of Cheerios.

It's time to say goodbye right now
So I guess I'll just say chow!

Eimear Campbell (11)
St Mary's High School, Lurgan

Leaves

How silently they tumble down
And come to rest on the ground
To lay a carpet, rich and rare,
Just as soft as a teddy bear,
Going to sleep, their work is done
Colours gleaming in the sun.

At other times, they wildly fly
Until they nearly reach the sky.
Red, green, orange and brown
Leaves swishing from town to town.
In the end they fall asleep,
Thinking of fluffy sheep.

Sarah Campbell (12)
St Mary's High School, Lurgan

Autumn

Autumn is the time of year
For all the falling leaves,
Different colours
Dance on the ground
Like yellow, brown, orange and red.
Halloween, all the scary
Trick or treats,
All the costumes hunting
The different streets.

Athena Donnelly (11)
St Mary's High School, Lurgan

My Cat

My cat is called Lucky
And his favourite food is Kentucky.

He sleeps in a shed,
He might have a sore head.

Lucky would play in the autumn leaves
And when he's done he would leave.

He has one ear up and the other down,
But will never frown.

In the sun he would play and run
But especially have fun.

Lucky is black and white
And would chase a kite.

It's good Lucky will stay
And that's all I have to say.

Katie Catney (11)
St Mary's High School, Lurgan

No Man

The day was long and hard
Finally he reached his front yard.

He put a brave face on
And thought about what went wrong.

With no one to save him,
The world looked so grim.

Always in a fight,
Will it ever be right?

He is so full of madness . . .
This feeling is sadness.

Ellie Comac (11)
St Mary's High School, Lurgan

Winter

Now winter is the season
When the temperature drops very low
And then it seems for no positive reason
The weather changes from sun to snow.

Wrapped up warm from head to toe
Ready to go out for a walk in the snow
Slippery and icy is the snow underneath
Crisp and crunch is the sound beneath my feet.

It's fun to go out in just for a while
To see all the snowmen always makes me smile
And then I crunch home for a warm cup of tea
And think of all things wintry while I put up my Christmas tree.

Caitlin Seeley (11)
St Mary's High School, Lurgan

Halloween Night

As darkness falls, the children come out,
They skip joyously through the streets.
Dressed in costume, they laugh and shout
In search of tricks or treats.

From door to door they sing their song
And fill their bags with delights.
You had better not keep them waiting too long,
They will fill you with fear and fright.

Ghosts, goblins and gremlins too,
A terrifying display of creatures.
Behind every corner they are waiting for you,
They horrify with their disgusting features.

The full moon shines silently in the midnight sky,
From a distance you can hear a wolf howl.
The cackle of witches on their brooms up high,
Their cauldrons full of things most foul.

The drip of blood from the vampire's fangs,
He has another victim in his sight.
The watchful pumpkin from the window hangs,
Beware . . . it's Halloween night.

Emily Dowds (12)
St Patrick's Academy, Lisburn

Motto Poems

Motto: Live like there's no tomorrow!

Live each day like it's your last . . .
Do not live in the past!
There's no point in regrets -
They will only make you upset!

Keep smiling all day long,
No matter what may be wrong!
So just stay cool
And live life to the full.

Motto: Every day is a gift, that's why it's called the present!

Yesterday's history,
Tomorrow's a mystery!
Today's a gift
So forget any rift!

Live for the present
And just be pleasant!
Be it Monday or Sunday . . .
Don't be sad, just be glad!

Shannon Barlow (13)
St Patrick's Academy, Lisburn

Werewolf

One night when all was dark
I carefully walked through the park
The swings were swinging
Though . . . with no one to push
Darkness and evil lurked in every bush

As I went deeper
To my surprise
There it was staring . . .
A pair of eyes
But this was the least of my worries and cries
Because within the bin something was living

It fumbled and twirled
Then crashed to the ground
Then all of a sudden it had been found
It was now very obvious
It now had become clear
With claws and teeth to devour a deer

I looked into its face
It looked into my eyes
I wanted to run
I wanted to hide
But my body didn't move
But then all of a sudden it jumped out
And started to groove
In fact it was the werewolf
From Micky J too!

It twirled about
It asked me to dance
I turned round and said, 'No!'
Then it aggressively pranced!

It got me to the ground
In the blink of an eye
With a claw and a bite
It left me to die!

Conor Quinn (14)
St Patrick's Academy, Lisburn

Halloween Night

Halloween is here again,
It's time for pumpkin pie!
There's tricks or treats for everyone,
And witches flying high.

Fireworks sparkle, bang and blow,
And light up darkened skies,
There's rockets, jennys, bangers too
And wonder fills our eyes!

If you are scared of bumps or creaks
And prefer the Easter bunny,
Then do yourself a favour, dear,
And hide indoors with Mummy!

Marie Therese Clenaghan (13)
St Patrick's Academy, Lisburn

My Motto Poems

I look around at all these fools
Talking, joking and breaking the rules,
Then I know that they are gonna get in trouble,
So I keep my guard on the double!
They walk so cool, as if that's it,
And allow no stranger near where they sit.
Every kid in the class wants to be their buddy,
But when people come and ask me why,
I just say that I have to study.

Motto: Be yourself, not others.

You tried really hard to learn for your test,
But in the end you were stressed!
Just remember to always try your best,
And don't fool around with your quest.

Motto: Always try your best.

Christy Cyriac (12)
St Patrick's Academy, Lisburn

*Young*Writers

Bullying

Trapped in a corner, nowhere to go
People laughing, pointing, teasing
Where can I go, who can I turn to?
The answer? No one.

It hurts, the pain of each punch that collides
With my swollen skin
This pain, it just won't go away, whatever I do
They don't understand
Thud, another stone smacked against my face
There they are, gathered around me like a pack of vultures
Waiting for their turn to get at the vulnerable
And weak victim.

Walking home along a busy road
This is the only way to relieve the pain
As I step out . . .

Some may say this was a sad end
To a boy who struggled to find happiness
In a cruel, cruel world.

Peter Baker (12)
Sullivan Upper School, Holywood

Poetry Matters - Northern Ireland

My Halloween Night

The wind whistling in the dark, dark night,
The howling of the old man's dog,
The air so cold it's nipping away at my toes,
I can't even see the faintest light.

I feel like a spider is creeping up my back
Ever so slowly,
As I feel like someone is following me,
And all the trick or treaters.

Then finally I see my house,
Looking so warm and welcoming,
All I can do is smile
As my Halloween night is over.

Courtney Dawson (11)
Sullivan Upper School, Holywood

Drum Kit

On my throne I sit
Playing my drum kit.

What a wonderful snare,
It makes people glare.

Should I buy a crash?
Or should I buy a splash?
From Yamaha to Pearl
I love to do a twirl
With my drumsticks
It all just clicks.

Luke Niblock (13)
Sullivan Upper School, Holywood

Friendship

A friend can come in all shapes and sizes,
Friends to me are like gold medal prizes,
They act like a pick-me-up for when you're feeling blue,
And are there for the laughs and the giggles too.

Good friends are those who don't run and hide,
Even when the going gets tough, they stay by your side.
My friends to me are loyal and kind,
Even when one gets mad, the rest don't mind.

And then there comes sleepovers, we laugh 'til we cry,
We stay up so late, the next day we wonder why!
Friendship is something that matters to me,
And I hope I still have fantastic friends when I'm ninety-three!

Sophie Frazer (13)
Sullivan Upper School, Holywood

Halloween

Halloween is the time of year
That makes you jump and shiver with fear.
May it be ghouls, ghosts, or even vampires,
You'd better set up some barbed wires.
Hush, hush, not a whisper or sound,
Or you'll be eaten by a bloodhound.
Run, run, but you can't hide,
There are zombies closing in on your side! *Argh!*
Don't go to sleep, as safe as it seems,
For Freddie's waiting for you in your dreams.
All they want is to hear you *scream!*
So take the risk, it's *Halloween.*

Andrew Cave (12)
Sullivan Upper School, Holywood

Winter

Waking up on a crisp winter's day,
Looking forward to my nice hot shower,
I can't help my constant yawning,
I'll probably be in the bathroom for over an hour.

Wrapping up in my winter coat,
Gloves, scarf and winter tights,
Head out the door and climb into the car,
Everywhere there are still bright street lights.

As I travel through the darkness I wonder,
Is it night or is it day?

Through the school day, the cold and the wind,
All my school work makes me tire.
When I get home, a hot cup of tea
And warm myself by a nice toasty fire.

Eryn McAvoy (12)
Sullivan Upper School, Holywood

The Final Thoughts Of A Mountaineer

Up here, on my own
I'm at the top of the world
Yet I feel at the bottom
Don't want to celebrate
Don't want to be happy
I just want to get back down
But I can't
No, no chance whatsoever

Up here, on my own
Christmas with snow
Lovely, some people may say, not me
Personally I would rather have Christmas at home
Turkey, tree, fire, family, nice and normal
Normal, I love that word
It implies normality
The exact opposite of now

Up here, on my own
The only reason I did it was for a senses of accomplishment
But the only thing I'm feeling is cold
Most people want to get up here
But I just want to get down
Every moment it gets a little harder and a little harder
Even just living seems more of a struggle
The concept of death seeming closer and closer . . .

Emily Boyd (11)
Sullivan Upper School, Holywood

Magic

It can act
It can play
It can shock you all day
It is fun, it's not dumb
It makes you want to come and play
If I asked you what it was
You might just say that's tragic
So this will surprise you a bit
In actual fact, it's magic!

Jonny Betts (13)
Sullivan Upper School, Holywood

Asbo

His eyes so bright like the stars above,
He comes running to me so full of love.
Cute and cheeky all rolled into one,
When he's around, I know I'll have fun.
He's my loyal friend and clever too,
And will always be forever true.
His coat is as shiny as can be,
My puppy, Asbo, is magic to me!

Kerry Patterson (12)
Sullivan Upper School, Holywood

The Fireworks Poem

Boom, crash, bang
The sounds that you hear
They light up the sky
Their colours oh so different
Blue, red, yellow,
Crazy noises, oh who cares?
It's the fireworks!

Tom Parsons (12)
Sullivan Upper School, Holywood

Magic

Magic is here,
Magic is there,
Magic is everywhere,
From the tallest mountain
To the deepest ocean.

Magic is in you and I.
When you get a feeling of that magic,
It makes you feel warm inside.
It gives you a tingly feeling,
You just have to find it first.

Magic is in the air you breathe,
In the food you eat,
In the clothes you wear,
From your hat down to your socks.

Magic is in a picture,
In a flower,
In your skin and in your hair,
In your eyes of the bluest skies,
In your nose, down to your toes.

James Gibson (12)
Sullivan Upper School, Holywood

This Is Simply A Poem About Poems

Poems should usually rhyme
You should say them in time
A poem is usually sour like a lime
Or as smooth as a chime
If it doesn't, it's not a crime
It's simply just unique
This poem may not be the perfect poem
It's just unique.

Rory Harrison (12)
Sullivan Upper School, Holywood

Sweet Shop

Long strawberry laces reaching down to your ankles
Fizzy sherbet that tingles on your tongue
Melt in your mouth caramels
Whistle lollies being sung

Soft marshmallows
Rainbow lollies bigger than your head!
Jelly babies in their kilos
Lovely crunchy shortbread

Smarties every colour under the sun
Bonbons in a pale, powdery pink
Haribo in the trillions
Liquorice Allsorts which really stink

Children laughing
The *ka-ching* of the cash register
The footsteps of happy customers chasing each other out
That's what a sweet shop is.

Medbh Henry (12)
Sullivan Upper School, Holywood

Steven Gerrard

Captain of Liverpool - legend,
It only takes this man a second,
Liverpool are shocking,
But Stevie is rocking,
So come on, Stevie, you've a gap to mend.

When this guy's not playing, we're done,
Whether it's six-nil, three-nil or one!
So don't go away,
You and Nando must play,
So Man U, you'd better run.

His footwork is so precise,
He makes other teams look like mice,
His skills, they're so rare,
People stop and just stare,
It only takes one throw of the dice.

He's famously known for his shots,
Everyone simply says, 'What?'
He is a top man,
He amazes all the fans,
He ties his opponents in knots.

This man is a legend to me,
Like him I aspire to be,
I'm his number one fan,
He's a magnificent man,
He is simply fantastic, you see.

Andrew Bell (12)
Sullivan Upper School, Holywood

Dreams

My dreams in my head
Appear when I go to bed,
Sleeping, nice and warm I stay,
Images then they do array.

People that I've never seen,
Asking me where I have been.
I play with animals beyond my mind,
And many plants I do find.

I lie in fields of Jelly Tots
And watch the sky with clouds like dots,
And wander through a land of ice,
With skiing things that look like mice.

I want to stay here forever,
But I know that it will happen never,
'Cause when I wake it will all be over,
A dream that I will not remember.

I say goodbye to the strange creatures,
And tell that there is a reason
For me having to go so soon
And gaze up at the purple moon.

Next thing I hear is my mother calling,
She told me the dream was appalling,
And to go to school and she started laughing,
So here I am and the whole class is clapping.

Zoë Gibson (12)
Sullivan Upper School, Holywood

My Piano

The introduction sounds.
The smoothness of the keys beneath my fingers
Feels like soft silk stroking my hands.
Touching the notes delicately,
The dynamics flow from the instrument,
In a mixture of angriness and softness.
In a crescendo I take the scale to its full pitch,
Then with a sweet flurry of a trill, I creep back down again.
The tempo slows,
Loud chords splutter out.
A subtle pause in the calamity,
Then the bass notes creep in.
Arpeggios fly up and down,
As the left hand commandeers the melody,
Furiously hammering out the sound,
Portraying the emotion and passion of the music.
The left hand stops,
The right hand drifts up and down the keys wistfully.
Some more, subtler chords sound,
Signifying the end of the piece.

Annie McQuoid (12)
Sullivan Upper School, Holywood

Everything's Magic

Magic is the forest where the wildflowers grow,
Enchanted and mysterious,
But no one dares go.

Magic is the cave where the great beast sleeps,
With the treasures and corpses
And horrors it keeps.

Magic is the sea, so vast and pristine,
What wonders await beneath
Its radiant gleam?

Magic is the kingdom where people do stay,
Where witchcraft and sorcery
Banish goodness away.

Magic is just about anywhere you look,
You could watch a movie
Or open a book.

Patrick Moorhead (12)
Sullivan Upper School, Holywood

The Photo

I have this photo of me and my nan,
Our smiles are as big as they possible can,
There are flowers all around us as pretty as can be,
I remember this being taken when I was three.

We are standing there and she is holding my hands,
I noticed her top matches my hairband,
We are both squinting at the sun,
We looked for some shade but there seemed to be none.

Years went by and I thought of that day,
How me and my nan would just sit and play.
I think of how proud she would be of me,
And how this picture will always be on my wall to see.

Emma Luke (13)
Sullivan Upper School, Holywood

The Figure

One night in the moon and the dark and the gloom,
Where the werewolves howl and the witches scowl,
When the clock strikes twelve and the demons delve,
Not where the fireworks crackle, but near where the old hags cackle,

A figure rushed out, all pale and stout,
It shrieked and it howled, it groaned and it growled.
My legs turned to jelly and I rolled on my belly.
I reached for my gun in the hope it would run,
But it lashed out at my head . . . as I woke up in bed!

Michael Parr (11)
Sullivan Upper School, Holywood

Sampson And Goliath

Steel so thick,
So big and tall.
Their grand days gone,
No boats made here anymore.
They'll carry on
Watching us
For years to come,
Standing tall.

James Stewart (11)
Sullivan Upper School, Holywood

The Wizard's Apprentice

A flash of light
From open palm
A cry of surprise
And all is calm

Man kneels before wizard
'Have mercy on me!'
All is forgiven
'My apprentice you'll be.'

As the wizard's student
The man was tragic
But he worked very hard
And now he's magic.

Robin Watts (12)
Sullivan Upper School, Holywood

Fear!

I awoke in the room
It was very small
It looked like it was getting smaller
It was.

I tried to push against it
There was no point
It kept on getting smaller and smaller
Until I was squished out of this world . . .

Only to wake up in a worse one!

There I was in a village
But not a very nice one
Unless you think werewolves are friendly
And Dracula is your BFF!

I wanted to get out of there
I looked cautiously for an exit
But I only discovered
That this world was getting smaller too!

I tried once more
To push back the closing walls
And to my surprise
The walls went back!

So I kept on pushing
Back the surrounding walls
Only to find myself
In the room that I started off in!

But this time
I could push back the closing walls!
So I started to do exactly what I had done
In the other world

But only to discover . . .
When I did
A door appeared out of nowhere!
So I walked outside
But what I saw was . . .

Another small room!

Harrison Bell (11)
Sullivan Upper School, Holywood

Halloween

There I am, curled up on my sofa
On the eve of Halloween
When the children call,
I would crawl up to my bedroom,
The sweat trickling down my sleeve,
As I would be pleased if they never came back again.
This is why I would never buy a costume or mask as such.
As I hear the bell, I start to feel unwell
And the words 'Trick or treat?' are to my dismay.
So now I must face my fears as I hear my mum say,
'Come down here, dear.'
I smile, while the pain of one thousand nails goes through my skin,
As if to say, 'A few more seconds until they're away,
It will be OK!'

Wajed Amin (12)
Sullivan Upper School, Holywood

Spiders

I'm not scared of the dark
And I'm not scared of bark.
I'm not scared of dogs
And I'm not scared of logs,
But I'm scared of spiders,
The way they scutter
And go up the gutter,
The way they get in your path
And the way they're always in your bath.
That's why *I hate spiders!*

Rory Jemphrey (11)
Sullivan Upper School, Holywood

Fears

Frightened of spiders
They run and hide
In dark places you can't find
So big and hairy
It makes them so scary

Dark, scary places
That are out of bounds
Hear the spooky sounds
They make my heart pound

The bright full moon
The tales that go around
Witches and wolves with their howling sounds
Is it all true, or will it come soon?
Maybe this year
As we all have a fear.

Calum Cowan (12)
Sullivan Upper School, Holywood

Fear

You don't know when it's going to strike,
Like a tiger waiting to pounce,
Ready to take your breath away,
Muscles tensed like coiled springs.

Clothes drenched like they've been dipped in puddles,
Heart racing like a Formula 1 car,
Your mouth is as dry as the Sahara Desert,
The screaming terror echoes inside your head.

Suddenly, bolt upright!
Wide-eyed, I realise
It was only a nightmare!

Jack Bruce (12)
Sullivan Upper School, Holywood

Midsummer

The sun breaks the darkness of night.
There is a slight chill to the gentle breeze.
Warm steam rises from the sweet-smelling soil,
Making the air thick and humid.
A layer of dew blankets the lush grass.
The birds chirp softly,
Filling the morning air with their soothing tunes.
Many distinct scents of flowers intoxicate me.
The water is calm
And slick as a glass mirror.
It is going to be a beautiful summer day.

Rachel Cormier (14)
Sullivan Upper School, Holywood

Alone In The Dark

I woke with a start,
It was really dark.
As far as I knew,
There wasn't a shark.

I looked all around
And I heard a creak.
I already knew
I couldn't be asleep.

Suddenly I thought
That I was being choked.
Then I realised
It was only just a joke.
Just my imagination!

Sarah Gordon (11)
Sullivan Upper School, Holywood

One By One . . .

One by one
The creatures come:
Ghosts and gremlins
Looming home.

These are the things
That dance around
My imagination;
It knows no bounds.

Screech and scratch,
Creak and crack;
Shivers and tingles
Race up my back.

My room is black,
Dark as night.
The clatter outside
Gives me a fright.

I smell my sweat
Dripping down my head.
It meets my lips;
Tastes like I'm dead!

Lucy Hollies (11)
Sullivan Upper School, Holywood

Bullied

I sit alone at lunch and break,
Waiting for those harmful words,
A little shove, a little shake.
Here they come, come to break.

They push, they poke,
Mean words are spoke . . .
They think it's all a joke,

But inside I hurt, inside I bleed,
There was no need for all the harmful words.
Suddenly the bell rings.
All those that sat and watched, got up
As Mr Clark sang things like,
'Get a move on,' or 'Hurry up!'

I gather my stuff and walk
Across the school's front lawn.

Zara Goldstone (11)
Sullivan Upper School, Holywood

Nightmares

Going to sleep,
I sweep the bedclothes over me,
Wondering what my dream will be.
Turns out, it seemed,
My dream was no dream at all,
But a nightmare had got me in its grasp.

I twisted and turned
In my sleep,
But I just couldn't wake,
Not even a peek.

I was scared out of my wits,
But then the lights came on
And then all my fears were gone.

I thought that night was very long,
But it turns out I was wrong.
It never was real at all,
It was just a nightmare I had.
It wasn't anything bad!

Alex Gibson (11)
Sullivan Upper School, Holywood

Lachanophobia!

I have a phobia, you may laugh, it's called Lachanophobia.
It's the fear of vegetables!

It does cause some problems because for example last week
In home economics we made soup,
The teacher said it was chicken (no vegetables mentioned)

I arrived slightly late to find a big pot of
Bubbling, boiling vegetables!
Of course I screamed, ran out the door
And jumped out the window.
To my dismay I landed in the vegetable patch!
That was the last thing I remembered.

I woke up in a hospital bed
With a doctor and three nurses crowding round me.
The doctor said, 'Son, are you okay?
You took a panic attack and passed out.'
I said, 'Yeah, I'm fine. I'm feeling much better.'

That is the problem with Lachanophobia!

Joe Higginson (11)
Sullivan Upper School, Holywood

A New School Term

Beep, beep, beep,
Oh, how I haven't missed that shrill, piercing sound at 7am.
This is it, it's the start of the new school year.

The rain is tapping against the window, winter has arrived.
The long, hot summer days are over.
My uniform is sitting out and ready.
As I slip on my polished, black leather shoes,
I feel a hint of nervousness,
But it is soon overcome with excitement.

As I brush my teeth
And take a glance in the steamed-up mirror,
I realise how much I have changed.
No time to stop and think!
I slam the door behind me and run off to catch the bus.

The corridors are buzzing with summer stories and memories,
But soon they will all be forgotten.
New teachers, new classes,
But most importantly new start.
As I rip open my break, I am happy to be back,
It feels like I have never been away!

Hannah Yeates (14)
Sullivan Upper School, Holywood

Forest Fire

Deadly smoke curls in the silent night sky,
Suddenly a bright orange flame appears.
It crackles and burns like an untamed beast,
Eating the forest like lions to prey.
Unmercifully robs creatures of homes,
Licks up houses and trees in just seconds.
The night is still, this demon unnoticed,
Unexpectedly chaos has arrived.
Fire trucks speed to the scene, sirens blaring,
Water flies through the sky like an eagle,
Then it is gone, only ashes are left,
Silence and darkness return to the night.

Sarah Long (14)
Sullivan Upper School, Holywood

Humans

Through the nature we weave and duck,
We adapt and conquer to live once more.
Our settlements spread out wide,
The first of us had to hide.
How much we have grown
Through millennium,
From a useless race to intelligence.
I look to the future
And the past,
To wonder how
We grow so fast.

Jack Torrens (13)
Sullivan Upper School, Holywood

A Rainbow

It is a sad, grey day
With the rain falling heavily
Listen . . . *pitter-patter, drip, drop*
Goes the rain outside my window.

Then, alas, comes the sun
From behind those grey clouds
But still . . . *pitter-patter, drip, drop*
As the sun cheers up the grey day.

Look to the horizon
Something magical has appeared
Quietly now . . . *pitter-patter, drip, drop*
An explosion of colour sweeps across the sky.

The rain has gone now
Leaving behind the magical rainbow
Wow . . . it's so beautiful
So near but yet so far . . . untouchable!

Joanna Gallagher (13)
Sullivan Upper School, Holywood

Magic Of Childhood

Magic is what makes the world go round,
Magic won't always be there for you,
So make your childhood a magical one!

Ewan Nelson (12)
Sullivan Upper School, Holywood

The Magician's Magic

The magician's magic
Is the magic for you?
He can pull a rabbit out of his hat,
He can trick you with this,
He can trick you with that.
A bag of tricks the magician can do,
A bag of tricks he does for you.
He can come on one special night,
He can give you a fright.
He can trick you with this.
He can draw your sight
To give you a fright.

The magician's magic,
Is the magic for you?
For friends and family too.
He can saw a lady in half,
He can split her in two.
He can do it to you.
What else can he do?
He can trick you with that,
He can trick you with this,
He will never get a kiss!

The magician's magic
Is for you and friends, and family too.
The magician's magic
Is his show.
He can trick you with this,
He can trick you with that.
He pulls many ribbons from just one hat.
He can do this and that,
But the only reason he does his tricks
Is to get little children to scream and cheer.

His money goes to beer
With his mates!
The magician's magic
Is his show.

James Stevenson (12)
Sullivan Upper School, Holywood

My Mother, The Teacher

My mother, a teacher
At the local primary school,
Gets out of her bed
All grumpy and drool.

She spends ages
On her luscious hair,
When really nobody
Gives a care!

At breakfast time
She makes the toast,
But on Sunday
She makes the roast.

She climbs into her car
And drives very fast,
Because she has got to
Make it in time for class.

She arrives at the school,
Tired and run down,
But she never ever
Makes a frown.

She walks into the class
And the kids start to shout,
One of them is telling his friend
Not to be a tout.

The first lesson of the day
Is the big test!
Everyone else is trying
Their best.

The bell rings for break,
Then for lunch,
As Mother gives
The air a punch!

One more hour till
Her nice warm bed,
Because today she is feeling
Rather dead.

As soon as the clock
Strikes three,
Mother jumps up
With glee!

She arrives back home,
All rotten and vile,
She decides to sleep
For a while.

When she wakes up,
It's the morning again.
Another day
With a pencil and pen!

Ross McKenna (14)
Sullivan Upper School, Holywood

The Worst Pet Ever

My dog is very big
In more than one way.
She eats like a pig
And has two meals a day.
But she's a little chubby,
She's also very hairy,
And when she was a puppy,
She thought everything was scary.
But even all this couldn't stop her being funny,
She can't help the way she is,
And underneath she's as sweet as honey!

Lucy O'Sullivan (13)
Sullivan Upper School, Holywood

Brothers

B rutish bugle blowing
R ugged rugby ravaging
O ffensively ordinary objects
T reacherous tussles
H ell-raising hurtful hitting
E nthusiastically enterprising
R idiculous rib-tickling jokes.

Fergus Jemphrey (13)
Sullivan Upper School, Holywood

The African Phoenix

The cold of night bites
And the sun of day cruelly burns
Their possessions lie on sand
Home-made, not bought across till
The deadly flame burns the phoenix.

This is poverty
The poor of humanity
They work and not play
They huddle tight together
To keep the darkness away.

Poverty is burning
But the new dawn means a new day
Sing, dear Africa
Let the lion hear your cry
Let Africa's phoenix rise.

Children sing, rejoice
Tear the veil of poverty
Raise everybody's voice
Dance the dance of life around fire
Watch the phoenix rising.

Thomas Johnston (14)
Sullivan Upper School, Holywood

My Sister

My sister is so nice, so pretty,
Then when alone with me is not so
Pretty nor nice. She's different with me
But I don't know why.

My sister leaves the dishes, yet when
Mum says, 'Who did this?' she smiles her
Huge smile and shines her bright blue eyes
And I get blamed instead.

My sister is so popular, all the teachers love her,
'She is so smart, she is so cute,' they say.
But what about me? I'm never told I'm smart,
Nor cute. I'm just her sister.

My sister is four and I am ten,
She's different with me because she
Tries to be like me and my mum says
I did the same with Kelly.

I don't mind if people talk of
How pretty and nice she is, because it's true,
But she still wants to be like me, her sister,
And I love her because she's my sister.

Hannah Jackson (13)
Sullivan Upper School, Holywood

One Winter's Day

One winter's day
I rode on a sleigh
Over the hill
Until I became ill
Home to bed
With a hot water bottle on my head
Tissues nearby
Why, oh why
Did I not wear a hat?
And so there I sat
With hot chocolate in my hand
Until reappeared the sand
Where now lays snow
With people going to and fro
Making snowballs
With no care at all
Why, oh why did I not wear a hat?
And still here I sat.

Jemma Speers (13)
Sullivan Upper School, Holywood

My Friends

My friends are always there when I am low,
When I ask them for help, they never say no.

They always give me lifts to places,
And they all do have lovely faces.

Sometimes we buy each other lunch,
And sometimes we make pancakes for brunch.

My friends and I do lots of things,
Horse ride, town, at sleepovers we sing.

I wouldn't change them for anything at all,
I love them too much, they're like my dolls!

Alisha Burrell (13)
Sullivan Upper School, Holywood

The Stupid Boy

There was once a boy named Chris,
He was smelly, bad and someone no one would miss.
He wasn't very bright and had lost half his sight,
There was once a boy named Chris.

This boy called Chris sat on a rock and after all he could talk.
He talked and talked to no avail,
This boy called Chris turned very pale
As he weighed the same as a whale.

He did not eat very healthily
As he was not very wealthy.
Mickey D's and KFCs.

Every night he had a fight,
But one night he couldn't fight
As he went out with no torchlight.

There was once a boy called Chris . . .

Andy Martin (13)
Sullivan Upper School, Holywood

Food

This is a poem all about food
In my mouth it tastes so good
Spicy and hot, sometimes not
And sometimes sweet and sour.

Food tastes so great
When I masticate
And taste the flavours
Upon my plate.

Chicken, duck, sausage, beef,
I like to chomp with my teeth
McDonald's, Burger King, KFC
This is what we like for our tea.

Toast, sweets and hot chocolate
In our mouths taste so great
And when suppertime is over
We fall asleep and our hearts beat slower.

George Patterson (14)
Sullivan Upper School, Holywood

Bad Stew

Has your mum ever cooked a bad stew?
Because I am here to warn you
About all the disgusting things that go in,
Like stuff from our neighbour's garbage bin.
Blue cheese, pencil shavings,
Worms, rats and toenail clippings.
Once I even found in there
Some of my old pet dog's hair.
Apples, bananas, left to rot,
All inside the cooking pot.
You might think to put in some rice,
But now, how about some dead mice?
Liquorice, garlic and fish guts,
Mud, insects and old peanuts.
So if your mum says stew for tea,
You'll know what's coming, thanks to me.

Jack Preece (13)
Sullivan Upper School, Holywood

My Brother, Ben

Brothers and sisters can be such a bother
My brother Ben's the worst
He messed up my room and broke my TV
But I'll tell you the other stuff first.

He plays pranks on me all the time
One went very wrong.
He dropped four stink bombs in my room
That left a permanent pong!

Now my room has no door,
As Ben broke the hinge
One day my best friend, Tilly, walked in
On me getting changed - *cringe!*

He uses my money to buy his school lunch
But that doesn't leave any for me,
My tummy rumbles for the rest of the day
Until I get home for tea.

I wish he'd go and get his own friends
And stop ruining my fun
I tell him to go and play somewhere else
But he threatens to tell my mum!

Every time I have my friends round
He finds something new to do,
Like showing off my dirty underwear
Or walking in on them in the loo!

I just wish I could have some peace
It really is such a shame
But although my brother's a little pest
I love him all the same!

Aimeé McConnell (14)
Sullivan Upper School, Holywood

Trevor's Pets

Hello, my name is Trevor
I have strange pets, some stupid, some clever
Some fat and small
Some skinny and tall
Some have soft fur
Some attack with a *grrr*
Some are quiet and are birds
Some are loud and live in herds

First of the pets is Leaves
He is tall and eats leaves from trees
Leaves has a long neck
And when he walks, he's a wreck
Have you any idea what he is?

Along comes Harriot
She is a parrot
She squeaks and squeals
And swings on the reels

Next, what can I hear?
A loud and fearful growl
And then I can hear a howl
He loves the moon
It's coming soon
We have run out of time
With a sigh
I must now say goodbye.

Conor McEvoy (13)
Sullivan Upper School, Holywood

Homework

In my school bag it hides,
Waiting for my hand to pop in
So it can pounce.

The teachers threaten with them,
The deadliest weapon they have,
Designed to exhaust and waste your free time.

We get a book of horrors,
To record how many we get.
They call it a homework diary,
And fill it in we must try
Or we will forget, and that is *bad!*

Lydia McQuoid (11)
Sullivan Upper School, Holywood

Ode To Indie
(A girl in my class)

I really love you with all of my heart,
It's like I'm paper beginning to tear.
It is like you gave me that extra star,
Your beauty is in you and everywhere.

Inside art you were the best with the paint,
I would always cheer at your triumphs,
Although I saw you and needed to faint,
I managed to sit with you in science.

I would think about you inside a plane,
I would shout you on the side of a boat,
I would dream about you inside a train,
I would engrave your name onto my coat.

I never really wanted to make this,
I just hope it will help you to notice.

Aaron Banyard (12)
Sullivan Upper School, Holywood

Song Of The Wind

I comfort the broken heart
And free the prisoner of normality
By whisking up their hair and clothes
In a wondrous whirlpool.
I greet the seasons one by one.

Singing, whistling,
Dance little one, dance to my music
As I catch your pearly beads
In my swirling wonder.
I'll help you to kiss the bare trees,
The crooked walls, the shivering gardens,
To embrace winter once again.
Mourning, wailing,
As I sing farewell
And bid your wintry dance goodbye.

The spring comes again.
I twirl the scented skirts of her
Little choirs, perched on
Lofty boughs overlooking the green
Of a new beginning.

Summer and I, the welcomed,
Balmy breeze, gently caress
The azure waves.

Autumn and I rob the kingly trees
Of their last remaining
Russet leaves.

I comfort the broken heart
And free the prisoner of normality
By whisking up their hair and clothes
In a wondrous whirlpool.
I carry the cries of the poor and hungry
Across deserts and oceans to closed ears.

Will this year be any different?

Rachel McDougall (15)
Sullivan Upper School, Holywood

In A Grain Of Sand

Upon the pebbles
Lies a monument.
A glimmering reminder
Against the darkness of day.
Blissfully unaware
Stand the cobbles of the shore.
With exterior dazzling,
Contents a wonder;
They forget.
To the sand, but a grain.
Within a citadel of consequence.
Interior residence,
A flaw against Man.
The feelings, to bottle up,
Literally. A strain unseen on
The soldier, alone, but -
A flaw I choose to take.
For when other days
Inhabit, there it lies
Upon the pebbles
Of a forgotten shore.
A golden memory, safe.
To take a sip is to
Be restored; infinite, for a
Brief flicker.
I sip.

And from that moment
I return to being.

Chris Moore (17)
Sullivan Upper School, Holywood

Summer's Midnight

When you wake up at midnight in the brilliant summer's moon,
You think it is morn or noon.
The bats in the air hunting their prey,
The owl, old, grey.
The mice in the fields tucked up with the cows.
In the midnight light, the cats fight
And the birds rest till the early morning light.
The night continues from nigh until dawn.
When the dawn strikes, the bats flee
And the animals wake up to welcome in the day,
And wave goodbye to the night.

Katie Ireland (11)
Sullivan Upper School, Holywood

Magic Poem

Harry Potter can fly
On his broomstick so high,
Wizards have pointy hats
And witches have black cats.

Ghosts are white,
Fairies are bright,
And owls only come out at night.

Halloween is there so you'd best beware,
Beware that it's there,
So you'd best take care.

Stuart Collinson (13)
Sullivan Upper School, Holywood

Rugby To Me Is Magic!

Glistening blades of grass
On a cold winter's morn,
My heart pounding with nerves,
My legs feeling heavy
But then the whistle sounds
And the ball soars high in the air.
Swiftly catching the ball
I sprint past one, two, three players,
Sidestepping to the left and then to my right
I see a gap in the hungry defence.
Swerving past another player
I'm through
I've *scored*
Now it's the final play.
There's a crack in the weakened defence,
It's me against a bombing giant.
As I brace myself to take the hit
I suddenly experience a huge burst of strength.
Lifting him off the ground
I hurl him into touch.
The whistle sounds and a joyous roar erupts
Sullivan have won the *School's Cup!*
This was the game of all games
Marvellous, magnificent, memorable
No, it was *magic!*

Callum Jeffrey (12)
Sullivan Upper School, Holywood

Magic Is The World

Magic is a trick of the mind,
A fantastic ability.
The way the footballer takes on the defender,
The way he moves the ball.

Magic is also our life,
The world we live in,
The creatures, nature and of course ourselves.

Magic goes out to long romantic relationships
That can't be broken.
The way people meet in a dusty alleyway
Or in a bar, whatever makes you smile.

Magic is wizards,
Those have secrets to keep.
Spells, fantasy and the tricks
They do for our enjoyment.

Magic is something to startle you.
How the goal was scored,
When trees grow,
The love when relationships begin,
How the wizards perform tricks.

Magic for me is the world on its own.

Adam McAllister (12)
Sullivan Upper School, Holywood

The Magic Of Dawn

Darkness all around,
Silhouettes of looming trees,
The cold night air is frosty,
Suddenly - a flash!
Warm rays of sunshine
Filter through the trees,
Dewdrop crystals sparkle in the sunlight
Sending thousands of rainbows scattering.

The forest is alive.
Birds fly to their nests
Singing their sweet songs,
Spiders build new silky webs,
Rabbits hop around playfully
And deer nurse their young.
Pixie dust shimmers through the air,
The tinkling laughter echoing.
Invisible fairies dance
Springing from flower to flower.
The forest is truly magic.

Grace Douglas (13)
Sullivan Upper School, Holywood

Before Midnight Strikes

On Halloween night
The wizards and witches gather.
Their steamy cauldrons bubble
As they cast their spells.

The grimoire flicks open
As the wind whistles through the trees
And black robes rustle
In the autumnal breeze.

Bats squeak and rats scurry
In the rusty leaves of the undergrowth.
The echoes of spooky curses
Hang heavily in the air.

The clock strikes midnight.
There is silence at last.

Jennie Pitt (12)
Sullivan Upper School, Holywood

Magic

Magic is a wonder
In everything around us
It exists in the past,
The present
And the future
From the witch's brew
To the wizard's spell
Magic is my life
And I shall honour it
Magic is a wonder.

Magic is amazing
Magic is in everyone
It is in all our friends
Enemies
And families
From the poorest child
To the richest man
Magic is my world
And I shall respect it
Magic is in me!

David Anderson (13)
Sullivan Upper School, Holywood

Nightmares!

Click! as I turn out my light.
As I put my head to my pillow,
I wonder what dreams I'll have tonight!

I hope not nightmares,
I hate it when I have a nightmare,
I wish they were like sweet éclairs.

I wake up next morning thinking of my dream,
It was so nice,
Like chocolate ice cream!

Jessica Chrishop (12)
Sullivan Upper School, Holywood

Young Writers Information

We hope you have enjoyed reading this book - and that you will continue to enjoy it in the coming years.

If you like reading and writing poetry drop us a line, or give us a call, and we'll send you a free information pack.

Alternatively if you would like to order further copies of this book or any of our other titles, then please give us a call or log onto our website at www.youngwriters.co.uk

Young Writers Information
Remus House
Coltsfoot Drive
Peterborough
PE2 9BF
(01733) 890066